Super Suppers
SOUP, SALAD & PASTA

Bon Appétit

bouillon

3 half
chicken
breasts

bay leaf

thyme

Bon Appétit

Super Suppers
SOUP, SALAD & PASTA

A collection of recipes
by Ursel Norman
Designed and illustrated by Derek Norman

BOOK CLUB ASSOCIATES
LONDON

Contents

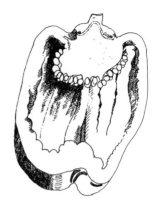

This edition published 1982 by
Book Club Associates
By arrangement with Wm. Collins Sons and Company Ltd

Printed in Spain by Graficromo, S.A.

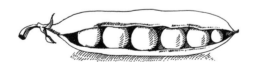

SOUP CONTENTS

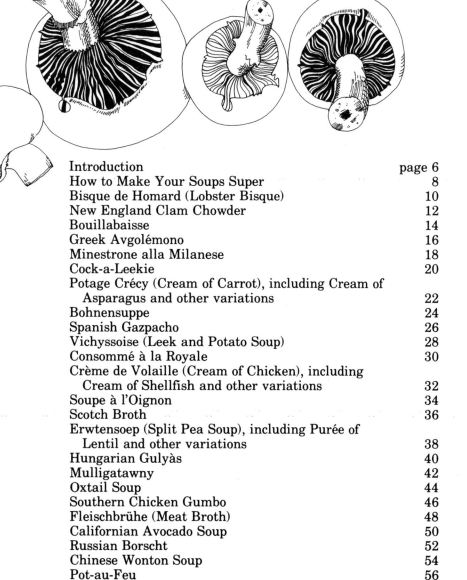

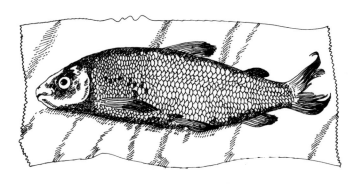

INTRODUCTION

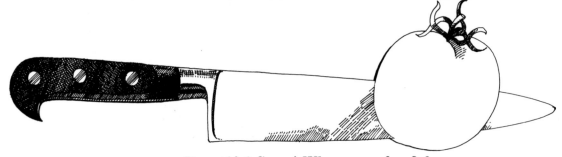

Beautiful Soup! Who cares for fish,
Game, or any other dish?
Who would not give all else for two
    pennyworth only of beautiful Soup?
Beau-ootiful Soup!
Beau-ootiful Soup!
Soo-oop of the e-e-evening,
Beautiful, beauti-FUL Soup!

This famed piece from *Alice in Wonderland* by Lewis Carroll
is but a taste of the wealth of poetic language that has helped
immortalize soup. For centuries soup has given inspiration to
peasants and poets, and sent gourmets into lyrical raptures.
For soup is a dish to stimulate the imagination and whet the
appetite. As one early 20th-century gourmet put it: 'There
is nothing like a plate of hot soup, its wisp of aromatic steam
making the nostrils quiver with anticipation . . . one whiff of a
savoury, aromatic soup and appetites come to attention.'
 Soup has historically played a highly significant part in
human existence, for it was a basis for nourishment and
survival. The cauldron was the original stockpot and provided
an everchanging broth enriched daily with whatever
ingredients happened to be available.
 Such simple peasant fare gave birth to the earliest of the
many national soups, many of which fortunately survive. For
every country there was virtually a national soup, their
preparation being somewhat similar but differing by virtue of
their ingredients which reflected regional and national tastes.
Some of the most famous are Pot-au-Feu from France,
Minestrone from Italy, Borscht from Russia, Gazpacho from
Spain and Erwtensoep from Holland.
 Within this book you will find all these soups, together with
many more, each with its classic flavours representing some
of the finest of European and American soups. All have their
individual tastes, aromas and rich historical associations.
Their different characteristics reflect the gastronomic cultures
from which they originate, tastes never to be found in any
tin although easily and inexpensively produced within the
confines of any kitchen.

Escoffier, in his famous *Guide Culinaire,* divides soups into two leading classes: '1) Clear soups, which include plain and garnished consommés. 2) Thick soups, which comprise the Purées, Veloutés and Creams.' The first class are clear meat or poultry broths, frequently served with some kind of dainty garnish. The second class of soups is made with some kind of starchy ingredient, producing cream soups of various kinds. There is a third type of soup, usually a main-dish soup, like, for instance, Erwtensoep, Minestrone or Gumbo. These fall somewhere between the first two categories. There are many examples of all three categories within the pages of *Soup, Beautiful Soup.*

It is our sincere hope that the reader will be inspired to make extensive use of the recipes within these pages and that the very thought of homemade soup will send the cook scuttling into the kitchen!

We trust that both the style and content of this book do more than justice to the subject of soups, and that the Look & Cook format will prove a useful and practical tool in the kitchen. For it is designed so that the reader can comprehend at a glance how a dish is prepared and how it should look when it reaches the table.

Finally, we owe a debt of gratitude and thanks to all our tasters, on both sides of the Atlantic, who have kindly helped us appraise the taste and quality of all the recipes in this book. We hope the reader will find them as tantalizing as we do, proving to be feasts for the eye as well as for the palate! For what can be better, or bettered, than:

'Soo-oop of the e-e-evening,
Beautiful, beauti-FUL Soup!'

HOW TO MAKE YOUR SOUPS SUPER

Some Do's and Don'ts

Stocks

Almost all the recipes in this book use stock as the cooking liquid. Only when a large amount of meat and bone is used will water do. The best stocks of course are the ones you make yourself (recipes page 62). And if you have the time, do try them. The soup can only be as good as the ingredients that you put in – a good stock is half the battle.

However, tinned stocks or bouillon cubes can be substituted as long as you remember that the latter are usually highly seasoned, so go carefully on other seasoning, salt especially.

Skimming

Most soups throw up a lot of frothy scum just before they come to the boil. This ought to be skimmed off as best you can. It helps to give the soup a fresh, clear, clean taste and colour.

The best skimming tool is a soup ladle. Dip the ladle in a basin of cold water, shake dry, then dip it straight down into the soup (or stock) but *only just* below the surface, and skim off any froth that accumulates at the sides of the pot. Rinse the ladle in the basin of cold water before repeating the process. Further scum will also be thrown against the sides of the pot, so keep skimming just the sides. Skim, rinsing the ladle frequently, until the scum ceases to appear.

Degreasing

Degreasing is done in much the same way as skimming. Only when there is little fat left on the surface, and skimming gets too difficult, can you use a spoon to lift off the remaining 'eyes'. If you have trouble getting them out, run a paper towel across the surface quickly to mop up some of the grease. No soup – indeed no food – should ever appear on the table with a film of fat on it. One easy way to get it off is to let the soup get cold in the refrigerator. The cold will harden the fat on the surface and you can lift it off easily.

Soup Meats

The best meats for soups are those with bones, whether beef, lamb or chicken. These are usually the most inexpensive ones too, and they don't suffer from the long cooking.

Soup Vegetables

Many, many vegetables are used in soup making. But apart from those which give the soup its name and taste, there are the 'aromatic' vegetables that appear in almost all soups: onions, carrots and celery. Their flavour is greatly enhanced if they are sautéed in a little butter or margarine before being added.

Soup Pots

A good soup pot is a large, heavy-bottomed aluminium pot with a lid. Rather taller than wide, of about a 6-litre (10-pint) capacity.

Thin, light aluminium pots with a thin bottom and sides are unsuitable since they are bound to burn the longer cooking soups.

If you do not possess such a pot – and they are not cheap – do invest in one. You'll find lots of other uses for it, like cooking pasta or large amounts of greens, corn-on-the-cob, etc.

Covering the Pot

Very frequently in this book you will find the term 'partially covered'. This means that the lid should be set askew *just* a little, leaving only a tiny crack open. The escape of moisture will be minimal since most of it will accumulate on the underside of the lid and drop back into the pot. The reason for doing this is to stop the soup from boiling too rapidly – and to stop the lid from rattling. If 'uncovered' is mentioned, this is done to concentrate the flavours through evaporation.

Straining

Some soups need straining at some point, either to remove certain ingredients or to be made absolutely smooth.

In most cases the use of a fine-mesh strainer is sufficient. If a soup is too thick to pass through, use the back of a soup ladle to push it. This is far easier than stirring it around with a spoon.

In the case of clear broths or consommés, it is necessary to line the strainer with a damp cloth (wrung out in *cold* water). This dampening expands the fibres of the cloth to make it more efficient. This way even the smallest particles are held back.

Good straining cloths are cotton (not synthetic) that are easy to wash and keep clean. Top of the list are muslin nappies!

Thickeners

Most soups contain some amount of starchy thickeners. These can be flour, cornflour, rice or other cereals or potatoes. They are all neutral in taste and colour.

Puréed soups made from starchy vegetables (peas or beans) contain enough starch already and don't need thickeners.

Use of the Electric Blender

By far the most efficient way of using a blender is with the lid off. This of course is not practical all the time, especially when children are trying to get a peep at what is going on, but when all is quiet and peaceful, use this method:

With the motor in the off position, pour one soup-ladleful into the blender. Turn the blender to the lowest speed. When the contents are smooth add a second ladleful, then a third. When all this is smooth, turn to the highest speed and keep it there for a minute or two, or until the soup is absolutely smooth. Never do more than three ladlefuls at a time; overfilling reduces the blender's efficiency.

Flavour Enhancers and Food Colour

Absolutely none, ever, in anything! Food colours are quite unnecessary anyway. No food needs to look more yellow or more green than nature made it, and correct seasoning eliminates any need for flavour enhancers.

Freezing Soups

Nearly all soups can be frozen without any loss of taste or texture. If the soup looks lumpy after defrosting, a quick beating with a wire whisk during reheating will restore the smoothness. Guides to which soups can be frozen are included in the recipes.

450g (1 lb) raw lobster meat,
   fresh or frozen, cut into
   1-cm (½-in) chunks
1 medium carrot, chopped
1 medium onion, chopped
2 parsley stalks, chopped
75g (3 oz) butter
½ teaspoon dried thyme
1 bayleaf
25 ml (1 fl oz) brandy
100 ml (4 fl oz) white wine
generous litre (2 pints) chicken
   stock *or* bouillon
75g (3 oz) long grain rice,
   uncooked
generous 500 ml (1 pint) water
50g (2 oz) unsalted butter
50 ml (2 fl oz) double cream
cayenne pepper
salt and pepper   Serves 5–6

1 In the pot sauté the chopped onion, carrot and parsley in the butter for 5 minutes. Add the thyme and bayleaf and sauté further until the vegetables just begin to brown.

3 Pour the brandy into a small soup ladle and ignite it by holding it over a gas flame (or use a match). When the brandy is actually burning, pour it over the fish and vegetables, shaking the pot vigorously until the flame dies down.

4 Then add the wine. Boil the mixture over a high heat until the liquid has reduced to less than half.

5 Add the stock and simmer the bisque, uncovered, for about 10 minutes.

6 Meanwhile, boil the rice in the water till tender (about 20 minutes). Add the rice and water to the soup.

7 Purée the soup in the blender until it is absolutely smooth. Strain through a fine-mesh strainer, discarding what does not go through. Return soup to pot.

8 Bring the soup to boil and skim as necessary. Also skim off any fat that rises to the surface. Boil, uncovered, until the scum no longer appears.

Just before serving, blend in the butter and cream and season to taste with cayenne, salt and pepper.

BUTTER

chopped onion

thyme

bayleaf

Brandy

Flame

ine

stock

COOKED RICE
& COOKING WATER

return to ← pot

Strain

LOBSTER MEAT

2 Add the chunks of lobster meat and stir them around with the vegetables until the lobster acquires a nice pink colour.

Note For Bisque de Crevettes (Shrimp Bisque) substitute 450g (1 lb) of shelled shrimp for the lobster meat. (Shrimp will need to be cooked an extra 5–10 minutes at stage 5.) For Bisque de Crabe (Crabmeat Bisque) substitute 450g (1 lb) of crabmeat for the lobster meat.

Bisque can be made ahead up to stage 7, and even frozen if necessary.

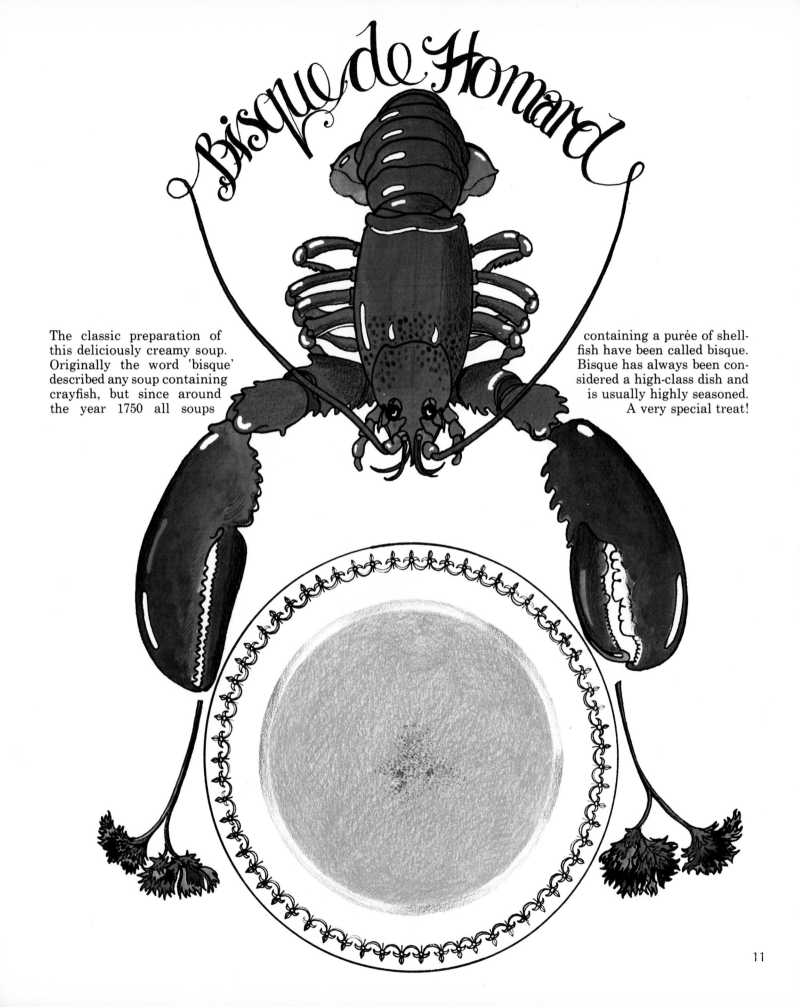

Bisque de Homard

The classic preparation of this deliciously creamy soup. Originally the word 'bisque' described any soup containing crayfish, but since around the year 1750 all soups containing a purée of shell-fish have been called bisque. Bisque has always been considered a high-class dish and is usually highly seasoned. A very special treat!

11

50g (2 oz) salt pork *or* fat
  bacon, diced very finely
2 medium onions, finely
  chopped
3 medium potatoes, diced
½ teaspoon dried thyme
generous 500 ml (1 pint) clam
  juice or water
485g (19½ oz) tinned minced
  clams and their liquid *or*
  2 dozen finely chopped raw
  clams and all their liquid
  plus generous 500 ml (1 pint)
  juice or water

generous 500 ml (1 pint) Jersey
  milk *or* half-and-half single
  cream and milk
50g (2 oz) flour
salt and pepper to taste
finely chopped parsley for
  garnish
little paprika for garnish

Serves 6–7

3   Now add the minced or fresh
    clams and their liquid, and the
    milk. Simmer, uncovered, for
    about 10 minutes.

4   Mix the flour with enough water
    to make a pouring consistency.
    Pour into the boiling soup slowly,
    stirring all the time with a wire
    whisk. Simmer, stirring all the
    time, for 3 minutes.
    Season to taste
with salt
and pepper.

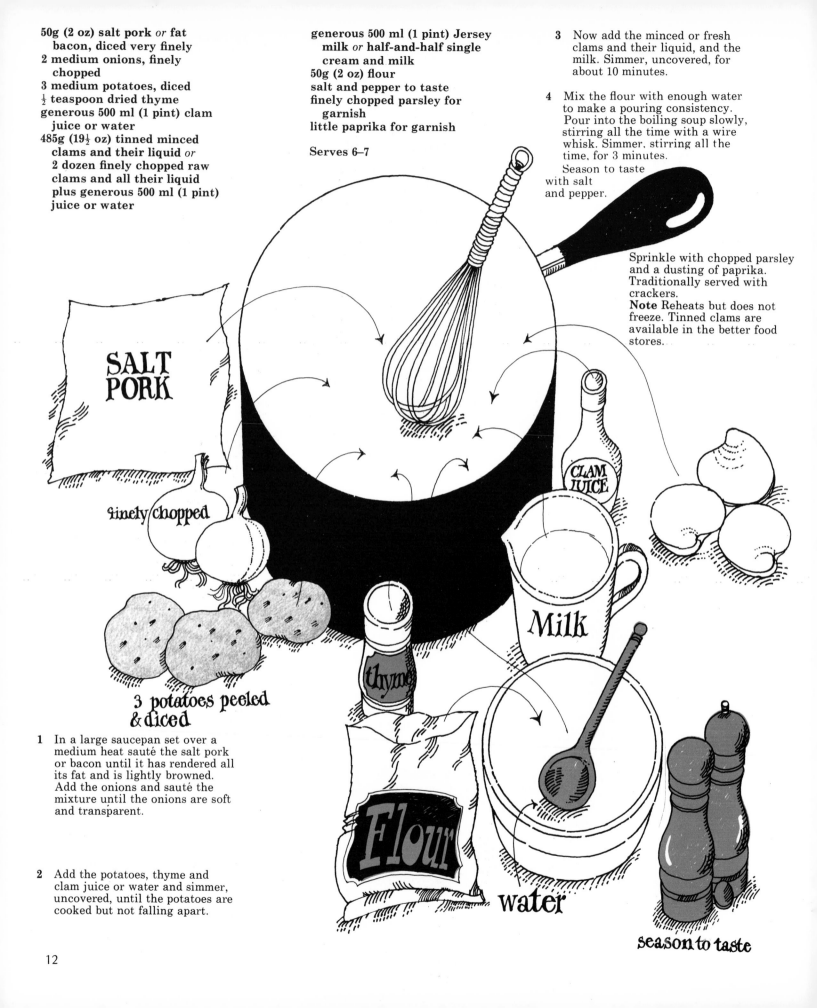

SALT PORK

finely chopped

3 potatoes peeled & diced

thyme

Flour

water

CLAM JUICE

Milk

season to taste

Sprinkle with chopped parsley
and a dusting of paprika.
Traditionally served with
crackers.
Note Reheats but does not
freeze. Tinned clams are
available in the better food
stores.

1   In a large saucepan set over a
    medium heat sauté the salt pork
    or bacon until it has rendered all
    its fat and is lightly browned.
    Add the onions and sauté the
    mixture until the onions are soft
    and transparent.

2   Add the potatoes, thyme and
    clam juice or water and simmer,
    uncovered, until the potatoes are
    cooked but not falling apart.

NEW ENGLAND CLAM CHOWDER

The name 'chowder' is derived from the French *chaudière* (literally, the fish kettle in which the dish was cooked), and was probably anglicized subsequent to French settlement in Canada. New England Clam Chowder is the most distinguished of all the clam chowders, with its characteristic clams, salt pork and milk or cream. Herman Melville immortalized the dish in his salty classic *Moby Dick*. 'Oh! sweet friends, harken to me. It was made of small juicy clams, scarcely bigger than hazelnuts, mixed with pounded ships biscuits, and salted pork cut up into little flakes, the whole enriched with butter and plentifully seasoned with pepper and salt.' The recipe here you will find a little more reliable, though guaranteed to rouse similar feelings. We feel sure Herman Melville would have approved.

1 kg (2 lb) fresh tomatoes, skinned and chopped, *or* equivalent weight tinned tomatoes
2 large onions, chopped
4–8 cloves garlic, crushed
2 sprigs parsley
1 bayleaf
1 teaspoon dried thyme
4–5 fennel seeds
2 pinches saffron
1 fresh or frozen lobster tail (shell left on and cut vertically into 5-cm (2-in) slices)
1½–1¾ kg (3 lb) various firm fish, cut into serving pieces (leaving the skin on some adds colour. Choose from: halibut, pike, cod or haddock
200 ml (8 fl oz) olive oil
1 teaspoon pepper
2 teaspoons salt

3 litres (5 pints) liquid, either cold water *or* ⅔ water and ⅓ white wine *or* fish stock from page 62
1½–1¾ kg (3 lb) various soft fish, cut into serving pieces (leave the skin on some). Choose from: mackerel, whiting, whitefish, flounder, sole, mullet or perch
12 croûtons (optional). These are slices of French bread, brushed with oil on both sides and toasted in a warm oven (165°C 325°F Gas 3) till crisp and dry.

Serves 10–12

1 Place the tomatoes, their juice, onions, garlic, parsley, bayleaf, thyme, fennel seeds and saffron into large soup pot.

2 On the bed of vegetables and herbs place the cut-up lobster tail and all the pieces of firm fish. Pour over this the olive oil, 1 teaspoon pepper and 2 teaspoons salt.

3 Cover the fish and vegetables with the liquid. Bring to boil over a very high heat. Continue boiling rapidly (do *not* turn down the heat), uncovered, for 7–8 minutes.

LOBSTER TAIL

FIRM FISH

fennelseeds

wine optional

SOFT FISH

water & wine (or fish stock)

4 Now add all the soft fish. Continue boiling on high heat another 7 minutes. Taste for seasoning.

To serve: using a slotted spoon transfer all the fish to a platter. Serve the broth in deep soup plates. Pass the fish separately. (If croûtons are used, place one in each soup plate first, then spoon the broth on top, then the fish.)

Note *Do not freeze!* This soup can be reheated with a minimum of stirring so as not to break up the fish.

BOUILLABAISSE

In a poem, 'The Ballad of Bouillabaisse', William Thackeray has helped immortalize this hearty Mediterranean dish. Bouillabaisse is generally recognized as having originated in Marseilles, although many areas in Provence claim to make the genuine Bouillabaisse. Try this Marseillaise Bouillabaisse, great with good company and hearty conversation. The Parisian version would also include mussels or clams. A rich spicy main-dish soup.

1¼ litres (2 pints) rich chicken
 stock *or* bouillon
50g (2 oz) long grain rice,
 uncooked
2 whole eggs *or* 1 egg and
 2 egg yolks
juice of 1 lemon
little salt (if needed)

Serves 4–5

1 Heat the chicken stock to boiling
point. Slowly stir in the rice and
simmer, partially covered, until
the rice is tender (15–20 minutes).

3 With a wire whisk stir this
mixture into the soup and,
stirring constantly, let it only
just come to boil. Remove from
heat immediately.

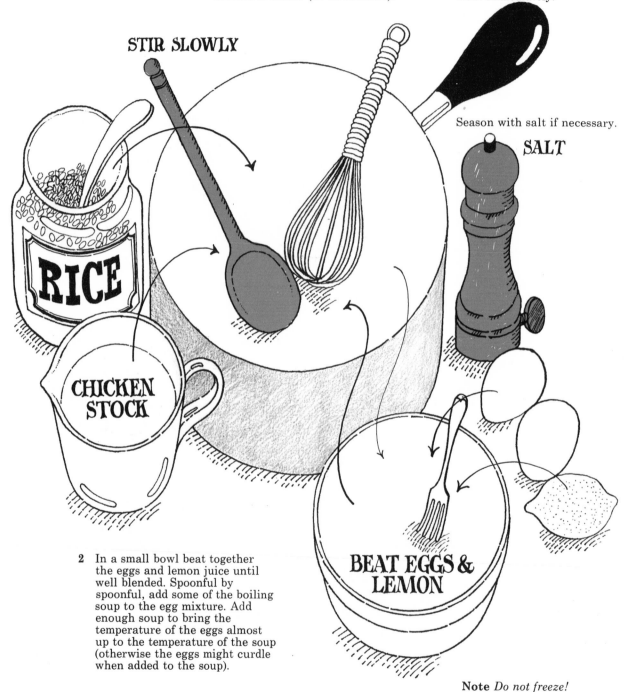

STIR SLOWLY

Season with salt if necessary.

SALT

RICE

CHICKEN STOCK

2 In a small bowl beat together
the eggs and lemon juice until
well blended. Spoonful by
spoonful, add some of the boiling
soup to the egg mixture. Add
enough soup to bring the
temperature of the eggs almost
up to the temperature of the soup
(otherwise the eggs might curdle
when added to the soup).

BEAT EGGS & LEMON

Note *Do not freeze!*

GREEK AUGOLÉMONO

The best known of Greek soups. Simple ingredients are combined to create a fragrant tangy flavour.

225g (8 oz) dry white beans, washed
5 tablespoons oil
1 large onion, cut into cubes
1 stalk celery, cut into cubes
2 or more cloves garlic, crushed
3 medium carrots, cut into cubes
225g (8 oz) fresh or frozen peas
225g (8 oz) unpeeled courgettes, cut into cubes
2 leeks, chopped (if available)
250g (8–10 oz) green cabbage, shredded
½ teaspoon dried rosemary
50g (2 oz) salt pork or streaky bacon, cubed
450g (1 lb) fresh tomatoes, skinned and chopped or equivalent weight tinned tomatoes, roughly chopped

2½ litres (4 pints) beef stock or bouillon
1 bayleaf
2 parsley sprigs } tied together
salt and pepper to taste
100g (4 oz) uncooked rice or soup noodles
5 tablespoons grated parmesan cheese

Serves 10

1 Soak the beans overnight in enough water to cover.

2 Cook the beans, covered, in the soaking water until tender, about 1–1½ hours. Add a little more water if they become too dry. Drain and set aside.

drain

3 Heat the oil in a heavy pan. Sauté the vegetables and garlic (if peas are frozen add them later), stirring often, for 10 minutes. Stir in the rosemary. Remove from pan and set aside.

SAUTÉ

ROSEMARY

oil

Sauté until crisp & brown

salt pork

drain

4 Sauté the diced salt pork or bacon in the same pan till crisp and brown. Drain on paper towel and set aside.

5 Into a large pot place the sautéed vegetables Stir in the tomatoes, beef stock, bayleaf and parsley. Bring to boil and simmer, partially covered, for about 20 minutes.

stock

skinned & chopped

6 Add the rice or noodles, prepared beans and pork, and the peas (if frozen). Simmer, partially covered, 15–20 minutes longer. Discard bayleaf and parsley. Taste for seasoning.

Pass the grated parmesan separately.

Note Reheats and freezes well.

Minestrone alla Milanese

An Italian classic with numerous regional variations. This particular recipe is a typical Milanese version, using rice as the thickener. Minestrone is to Italy what Pot au Feu is to France – it contains all the natural goodness and nutrition of fresh vegetables to give you a hearty main-dish soup.

1 Cover the leeks with cold water and sprinkle some salt over them. Leave to soak for 20 minutes or so. Rinse well; leeks are usually very sandy.

750g (1½ lb) fresh leeks, sliced ½ cm (¼ in) thick
about 2 teaspoons salt
1 small chicken
scant litre (1½ pints) chicken stock *or* bouillon
3 parsley sprigs ⎫ tied together
1 bayleaf ⎭
½ teaspoon dried thyme
50g (2 oz) pearl barley
200 ml (8 fl oz) double cream (or to taste)
salt and pepper to taste
chopped parsley for garnish

Serves 4

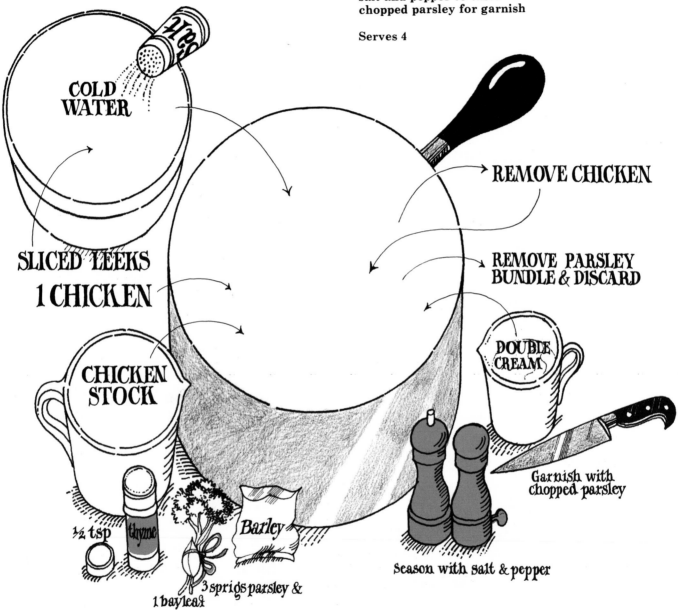

COLD WATER

SLICED LEEKS
1 CHICKEN

CHICKEN STOCK

½ tsp   thyme

3 sprigs parsley &
1 bayleaf

Barley

REMOVE CHICKEN

REMOVE PARSLEY BUNDLE & DISCARD

DOUBLE CREAM

Garnish with chopped parsley

Season with salt & pepper

2 Put the chicken into a large soup pot. Add the stock or bouillon, parsley/bayleaf bundle, thyme and barley. Simmer the soup, partially covered, for about 40 minutes. Then add the sliced leeks and cook another 15 minutes or so, until the barley is tender.

3 Remove the chicken and set aside. Lift out the parsley bundle and discard. When cool enough to handle, skin and bone the chicken carefully and cut the meat into bite-size pieces. Return meat to soup pot and heat through again.

4 Off the heat, stir in the cream and season well with salt and pepper. Reheat to just below boiling point. Garnish with chopped parsley.

Note This soup can be made ahead of time and reheated (or frozen) up to stage 3.

COCK-A-LEEKIE

As the name suggests, this soup was originally made with a cockerel. Nowadays chicken is a more than adequate substitute. A hearty main-dish soup – absolutely delightful on a cold winter's day, with good conversation and warm, crusty bread.

See! the smoking bowl before us,
Mark our jovial ragged ring!
Round and round take up the chorus,
And in raptures let us sing.
R. Burns

450g (1 lb) carrots, roughly chopped
1 large onion, roughly chopped
25g (1 oz) butter *or* **margarine**
generous 500 ml (1 pint) chicken stock *or* **bouillon**
25g (1 oz) raw rice
salt and pepper to taste
1 egg yolk
150 ml (6 fl oz) single cream
chopped parsley *or* **chives for garnish**

Serves 4

1   Sauté the chopped carrots and onion in the butter over a medium heat for 5 minutes, stirring frequently.

3   Put soup into blender and purée on low speed for a minute. Then turn to high speed until the soup is really smooth. (If the soup should be too thick for puréeing, add a little extra stock.) Strain through a fine-mesh strainer.

4   Return to pot and bring back to boil. Mix egg yolk into the cream and, stirring briskly with a wire whisk, stir it into the soup. Let it bubble up once or twice then remove from heat immediately. *Do not boil again.*

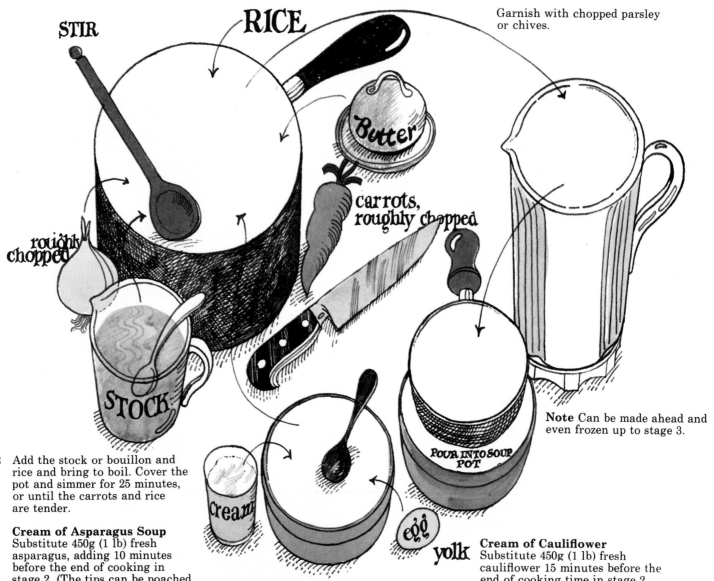

Garnish with chopped parsley or chives.

STIR

RICE

Butter

carrots, roughly chopped

roughly chopped

STOCK

cream

POUR INTO SOUP POT

egg yolk

Note Can be made ahead and even frozen up to stage 3.

2   Add the stock or bouillon and rice and bring to boil. Cover the pot and simmer for 25 minutes, or until the carrots and rice are tender.

Cream of Asparagus Soup
Substitute 450g (1 lb) fresh asparagus, adding 10 minutes before the end of cooking in stage 2. (The tips can be poached separately for 5 minutes and added to the soup for garnish.)
Cream of Celery Soup
Substitute 1 bunch of celery at stage 1.
Cream of Turnip Substitute 450g (1 lb) turnips at stage 1. (Some leaves can be poached for 5 minutes and added as garnish.)
Cream of Kohlrabi Substitute 450g (1 lb) kohlrabi at stage 1. (Some leaves can be poached for 5 minutes and added as garnish.)

Cream of Celery Root
Substitute 1 cubed celery root at stage 1.
Cream of Spinach Substitute 450g (1 lb) fresh or frozen spinach leaves 10 minutes before the end of cooking time in stage 2. (Traditional garnish is hard-boiled-egg slices.)
Cream of Broccoli Substitute 450g (1 lb) fresh broccoli 10 minutes before the end of cooking time in stage 2.

Cream of Cauliflower
Substitute 450g (1 lb) fresh cauliflower 15 minutes before the end of cooking time in stage 2. (A few leaves, blanched for 5 minutes, make a nice garnish.)
Cream of Fresh Peas and Lettuce Substitute 450g (1 lb) shelled peas and 1 roughly chopped round lettuce 15 minutes before end of cooking time in stage 2.
Cream of Brussels Sprouts
Substitute 450g (1 lb) fresh Brussels sprouts 15 minutes before the end of cooking time in stage 2.

22

Spinach Soup
A magnificent taste of spinach that would make Popeye proud! Fresh, appetizing colour.

Celery Soup
A fresh vegetable soup that can be enjoyed all year round.

crème de Céleri

Potage Crécy
(Cream of Carrot)
A simple, basic recipe that allows for all kinds of variations. Potage Crécy has a delightful orange colour, is mildly sweet and very creamy.

Asparagus Soup
Delightful – hot or cold!

Kohlrabi Soup
A creamy soup, with a delicate taste and texture. Very good hot or cold!

¾–1 kg (1½–2 lb) beef for soup (neck bones are good)
2½ litres (4 pints) beef stock *or* bouillon
450g (1 lb) runner beans, sliced diagonally
1 large potato, peeled and cubed
1 onion, chopped
1 carrot, chopped
salt and pepper to taste

Serves 6–8

1   Place the meat in a large soup pot. Pour on the stock. Bring to boil and skim off any scum that rises to the surface. Add onion and carrot and simmer, partially covered, for 1 hour.

2   Remove the meat and leave to cool slightly.

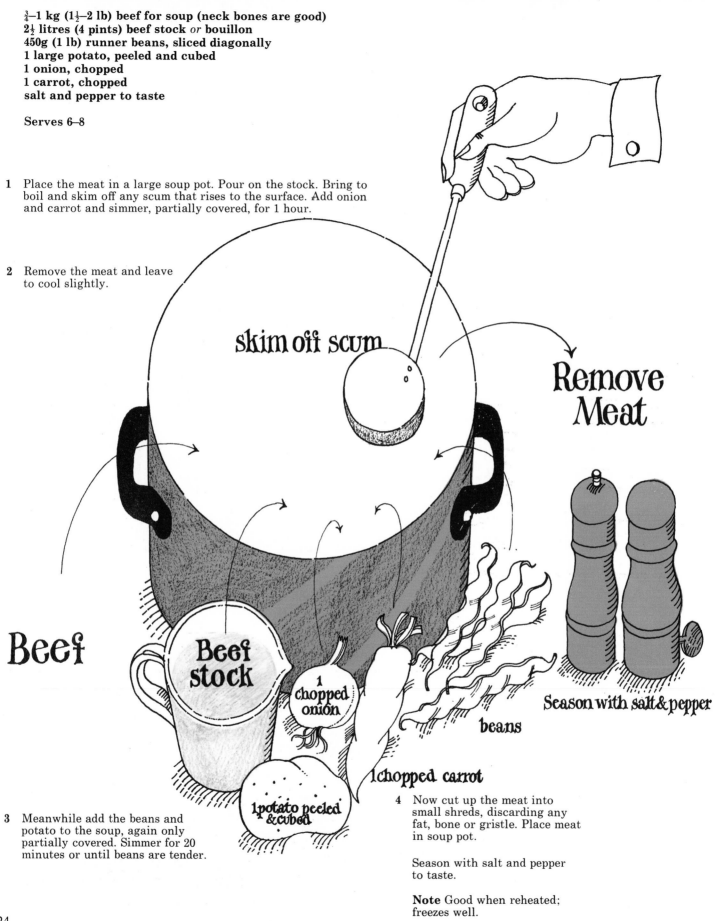

skim off scum

Remove Meat

Beef

Beef stock

1 chopped onion

beans

Season with salt & pepper

1 chopped carrot

1 potato peeled & cubed

3   Meanwhile add the beans and potato to the soup, again only partially covered. Simmer for 20 minutes or until beans are tender.

4   Now cut up the meat into small shreds, discarding any fat, bone or gristle. Place meat in soup pot.

Season with salt and pepper to taste.

Note Good when reheated; freezes well.

Bohnensuppe

A Westphalian soup that oozes a country earthiness. Honest and sincere, extremely low in calories and full of nutrition. Serve it piping hot for a fine lunch. A meal in itself, especially with crusty bread. Guten Appetit.

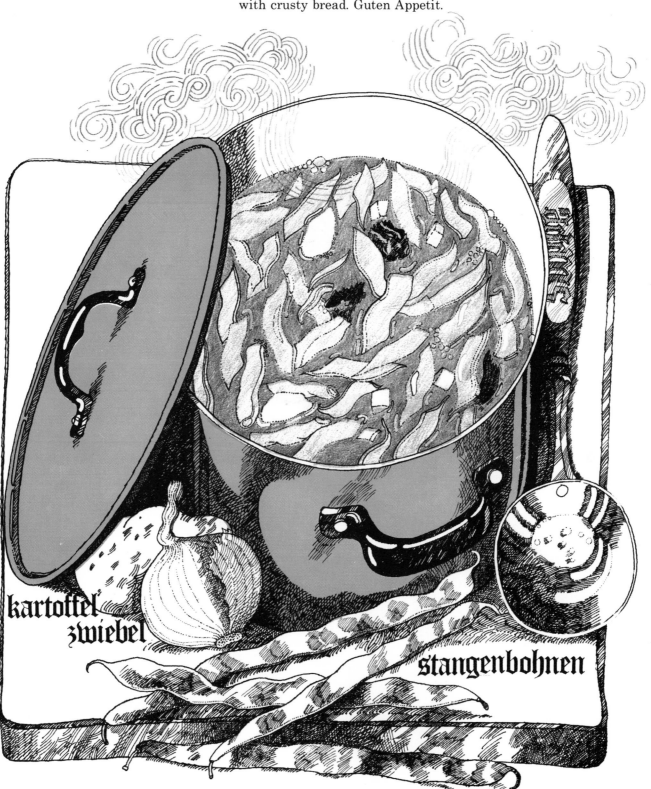

kartoffel
zwiebel

stangenbohnen

1¼–1½ kg (2½ lb) fresh tomatoes, skinned and chopped
1 small cucumber, peeled and chopped
1 clove garlic, crushed
1 green pepper, cut into strips
2 tablespoons tomato purée
1 large parsley sprig
150 ml (6 fl oz) cold water
4 tablespoons oil
2 tablespoons white wine vinegar
salt and pepper to taste
2 slices ordinary white bread, crust removed and cubed
2 spring onions, finely sliced
1 stalk celery, very finely chopped, and a few black
   olives for garnish

Serves 6

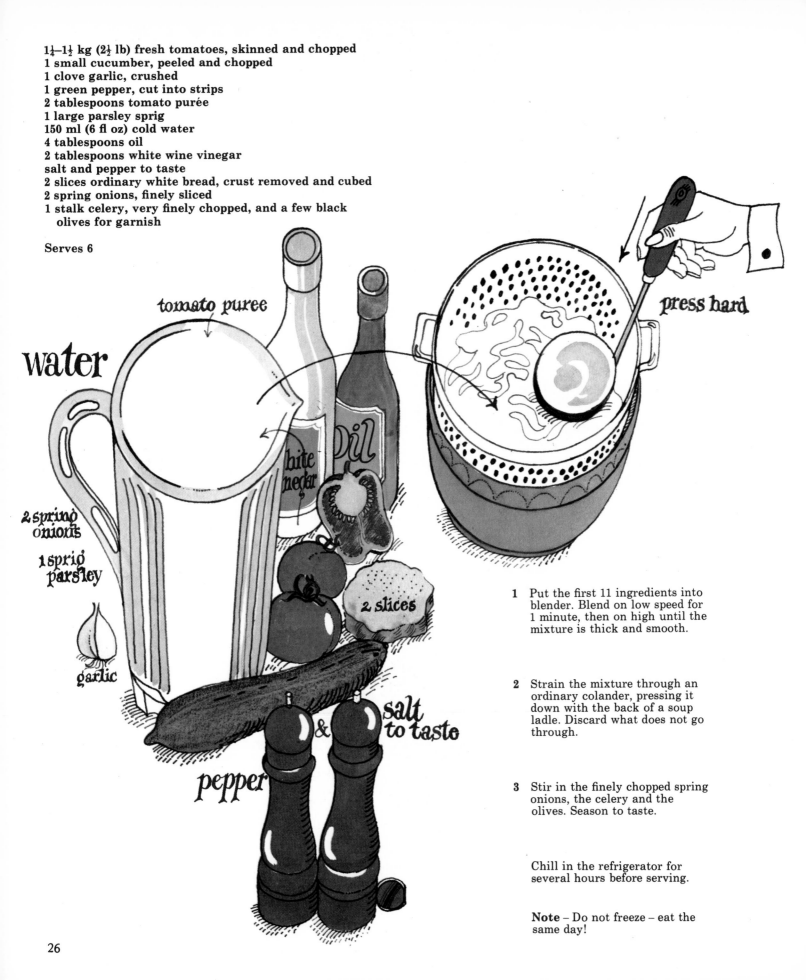

tomato puree

water

2 spring onions

1 sprig parsley

garlic

2 slices

salt to taste

pepper &

press hard

1   Put the first 11 ingredients into
    blender. Blend on low speed for
    1 minute, then on high until the
    mixture is thick and smooth.

2   Strain the mixture through an
    ordinary colander, pressing it
    down with the back of a soup
    ladle. Discard what does not go
    through.

3   Stir in the finely chopped spring
    onions, the celery and the
    olives. Season to taste.

Chill in the refrigerator for
several hours before serving.

Note – Do not freeze – eat the
same day!

SPANISH GAZPACHO

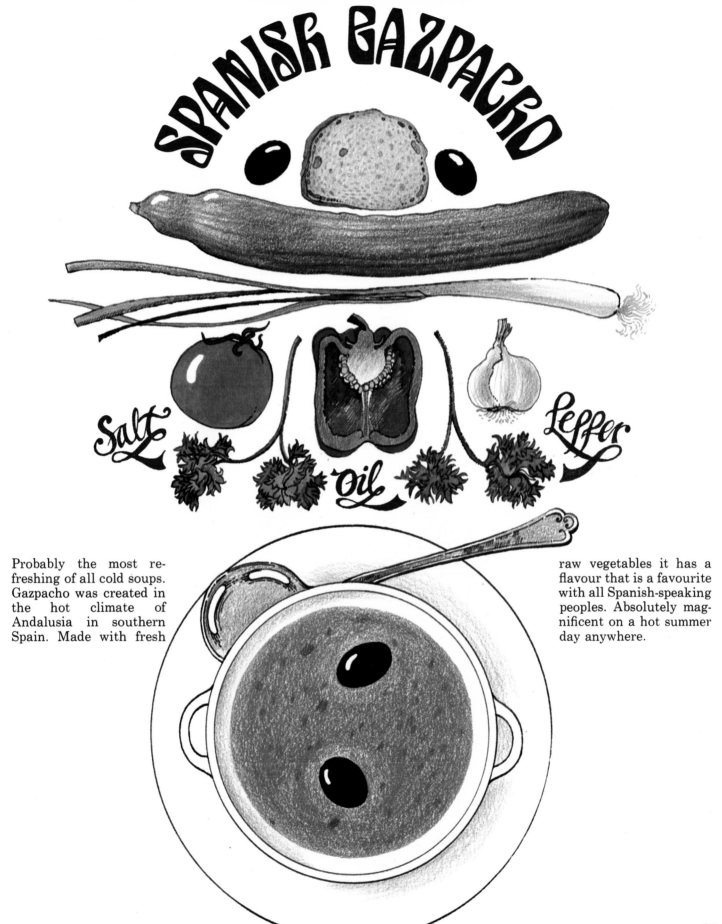

Probably the most refreshing of all cold soups. Gazpacho was created in the hot climate of Andalusia in southern Spain. Made with fresh raw vegetables it has a flavour that is a favourite with all Spanish-speaking peoples. Absolutely magnificent on a hot summer day anywhere.

Salt

Oil

Pepper

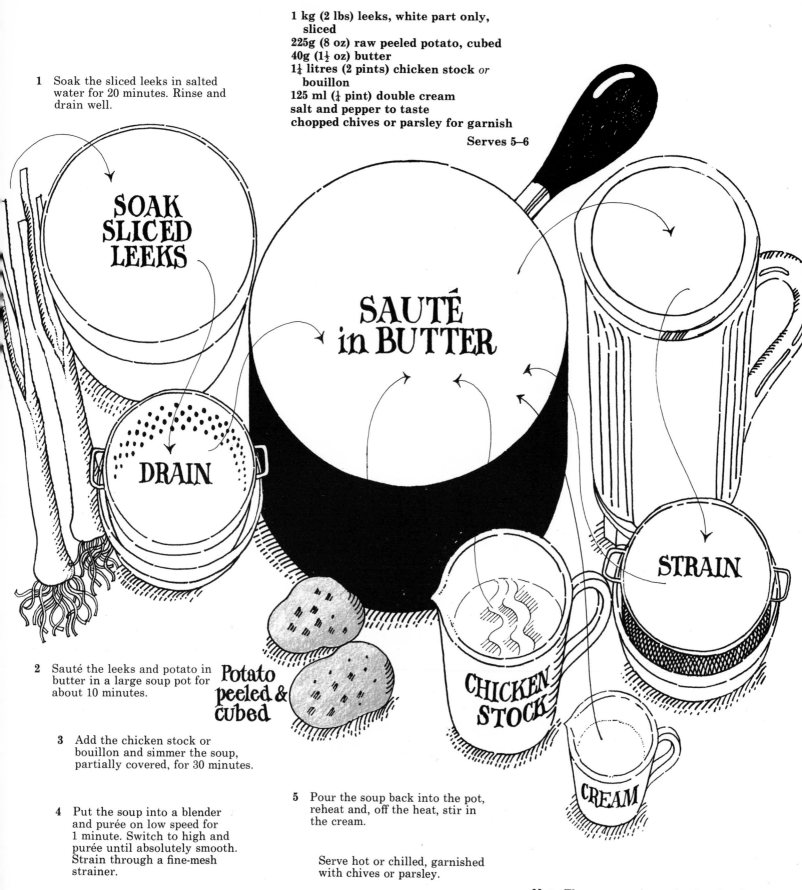

1 kg (2 lbs) leeks, white part only,
   sliced
225g (8 oz) raw peeled potato, cubed
40g (1½ oz) butter
1¼ litres (2 pints) chicken stock *or*
   bouillon
125 ml (¼ pint) double cream
salt and pepper to taste
chopped chives or parsley for garnish

Serves 5–6

1 Soak the sliced leeks in salted water for 20 minutes. Rinse and drain well.

SOAK SLICED LEEKS

SAUTÉ in BUTTER

DRAIN

STRAIN

2 Sauté the leeks and potato in butter in a large soup pot for about 10 minutes.

Potato peeled & cubed

CHICKEN STOCK

3 Add the chicken stock or bouillon and simmer the soup, partially covered, for 30 minutes.

CREAM

4 Put the soup into a blender and purée on low speed for 1 minute. Switch to high and purée until absolutely smooth. Strain through a fine-mesh strainer.

5 Pour the soup back into the pot, reheat and, off the heat, stir in the cream.

Serve hot or chilled, garnished with chives or parsley.

Note The soup can be made ahead and reheated or frozen up to stage 4.

Vichyssoise

Vichyssoise is a beautiful soup of fresh leeks and potatoes, and is served cold. There is no need here to do as Edward Lear's Young Lady of Poole:
> 'Whose soup was excessively cool,
> So she put it to boil by the aid of some oil,
> That ingenious young lady of Poole!'

(If Vichyssoise is served hot, it becomes Potage Crème de Poireaux.) Vichyssoise makes a fine, elegant soup for a formal occasion. Very delicate in taste and texture. Bon Appétit!

for the consommé
5–6 egg whites
2 teaspoons salt
½ teaspoon pepper
4 cloves
**1 kg (2 lbs) very, very lean
minced beef (the meat should
be from an old animal;
young ones yield very little
flavour)**
**200 ml (8 fl oz) red wine
(optional)**
2½ litres (4 pints) beef stock

Serves 6–8

for the royale
4 parsley sprigs
little salt and pepper
**125 ml (5 fl oz) consommé *or*
chicken bouillon**
1 egg
2 egg yolks

3 To the meat mixture add the cold beef stock
and then pour the mixture into a saucepan.

4 Bring to boil and simmer, uncovered, very
slowly for 2 hours, *never* stirring. The liquid
must simmer very gently, not come bubbling
through the meat mixture. Cook until the cake
that has formed on the surface is quite cooked,
with no traces of red.

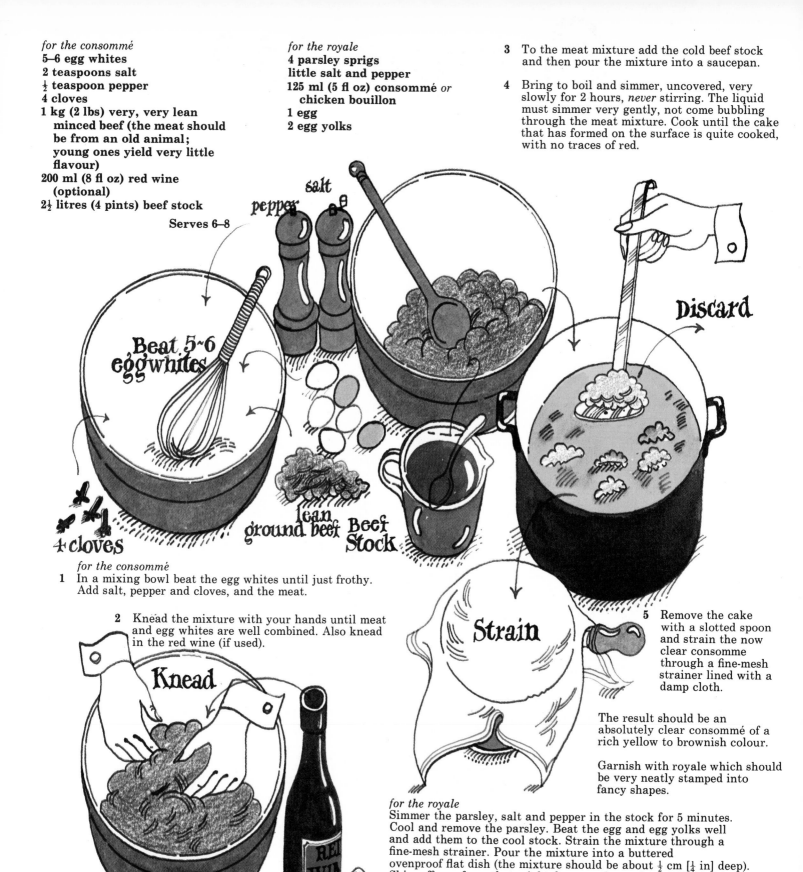

for the consommé
1 In a mixing bowl beat the egg whites until just frothy.
Add salt, pepper and cloves, and the meat.

2 Knead the mixture with your hands until meat
and egg whites are well combined. Also knead
in the red wine (if used).

5 Remove the cake
with a slotted spoon
and strain the now
clear consomme
through a fine-mesh
strainer lined with a
damp cloth.

The result should be an
absolutely clear consommé of a
rich yellow to brownish colour.

Garnish with royale which should
be very neatly stamped into
fancy shapes.

for the royale
Simmer the parsley, salt and pepper in the stock for 5 minutes.
Cool and remove the parsley. Beat the egg and egg yolks well
and add them to the cool stock. Strain the mixture through a
fine-mesh strainer. Pour the mixture into a buttered
ovenproof flat dish (the mixture should be about ½ cm [¼ in] deep).
Skim off any foam that might form on the surface. Fill a baking
tray with boiling water and set the ovenproof dish into it. Place
in a preheated warm oven (165°C 325°F Gas 3) for 20 minutes.
(Test for doneness with a knife; if it comes out clean, the royale
is cooked.) Cool in the dish before cutting.

Other garnishes for consommés
All garnishes for consommés have to be cooked separately, well drained and rinsed to keep them absolutely clean: julienned
vegetables, blanched 1 minute and rinsed; rice or noodles, cooked till tender and rinsed; leftover roast or boiled meat, cut
into julienne strips: quenelles or profiteroles.

Consommé à la Royale

The word 'consommé' literally means a perfectly refined soup. This recipe is a basic consommé garnished with 'royale'. There are numerous variations of this recipe, each largely differentiated by the type of garnish. Escoffier lists over 70 different kinds. Consommé, it is worth remembering, represents perfection, pure and exquisite. No rustic country character here. Beautifully clear, it stimulates the appetite as no other soup can. Perfect for formal occasions. A triumph of haute cuisine. Bon Appétit.

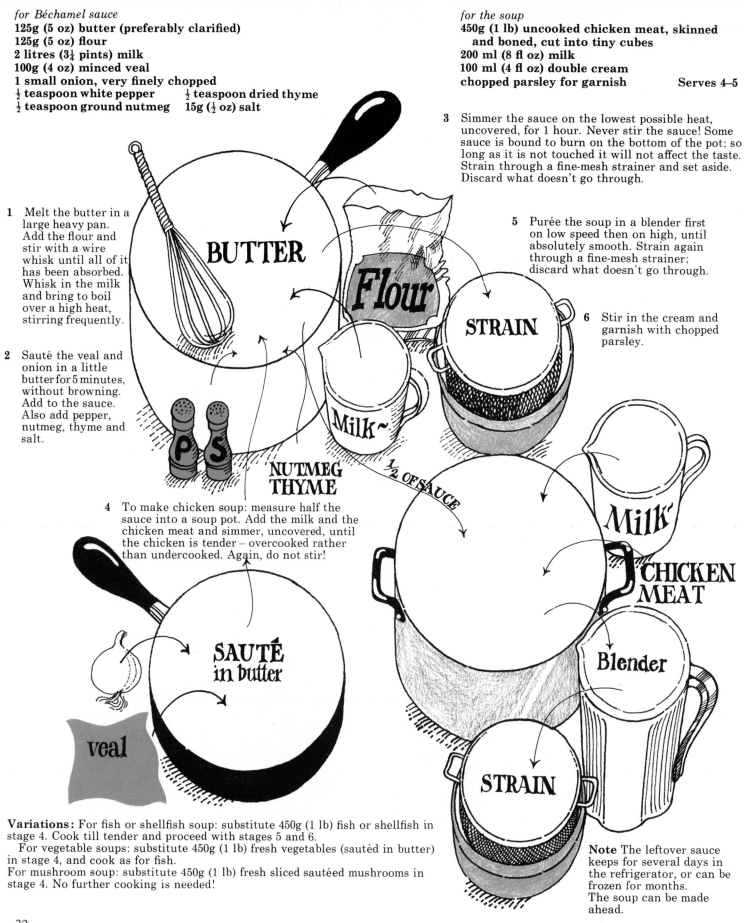

for *Béchamel sauce*

125g (5 oz) butter (preferably clarified)
125g (5 oz) flour
2 litres (3¼ pints) milk
100g (4 oz) minced veal
1 small onion, very finely chopped
½ teaspoon white pepper   **½ teaspoon dried thyme**
½ teaspoon ground nutmeg   **15g (½ oz) salt**

for *the soup*

450g (1 lb) uncooked chicken meat, skinned
 and boned, cut into tiny cubes
200 ml (8 fl oz) milk
100 ml (4 fl oz) double cream
chopped parsley for garnish   Serves 4–5

1 Melt the butter in a large heavy pan. Add the flour and stir with a wire whisk until all of it has been absorbed. Whisk in the milk and bring to boil over a high heat, stirring frequently.

2 Sauté the veal and onion in a little butter for 5 minutes, without browning. Add to the sauce. Also add pepper, nutmeg, thyme and salt.

3 Simmer the sauce on the lowest possible heat, uncovered, for 1 hour. Never stir the sauce! Some sauce is bound to burn on the bottom of the pot; so long as it is not touched it will not affect the taste. Strain through a fine-mesh strainer and set aside. Discard what doesn't go through.

4 To make chicken soup: measure half the sauce into a soup pot. Add the milk and the chicken meat and simmer, uncovered, until the chicken is tender – overcooked rather than undercooked. Again, do not stir!

5 Purée the soup in a blender first on low speed then on high, until absolutely smooth. Strain again through a fine-mesh strainer; discard what doesn't go through.

6 Stir in the cream and garnish with chopped parsley.

Variations: For fish or shellfish soup: substitute 450g (1 lb) fish or shellfish in stage 4. Cook till tender and proceed with stages 5 and 6.
 For vegetable soups: substitute 450g (1 lb) fresh vegetables (sautéd in butter) in stage 4, and cook as for fish.
For mushroom soup: substitute 450g (1 lb) fresh sliced sautéed mushrooms in stage 4. No further cooking is needed!

Note The leftover sauce keeps for several days in the refrigerator, or can be frozen for months.
The soup can be made ahead.

CRÈME DE VOLAILLE

Chicken

BRUSSELS SPROUT

Bon Appétit

This is the classic recipe for cream soup of any type. It is based on the extremely versatile Béchamel Sauce, and since it is a little time-consuming to prepare, a double recipe for sauce has been given.
This recipe makes a sinfully rich soup – absolutely the creamiest you will ever taste!

33

50g (2 oz) butter
450g (1 lb) onions, cut into thin
  rings
1 clove garlic, crushed
  (optional)
2 teaspoons sugar
3 tablespoons flour
scant 2 litres (3 pints) beef *or*
  chicken stock, *or* **bouillon**
125 ml (5 fl oz) white wine
1 teaspoon dried thyme
1 bayleaf
2 tablespoons dry sherry
8 slices French bread
100g (4 oz) grated Swiss or
  parmesan cheese
                              Serves 8

1 Melt the butter in a heavy
   saucepan. Add the sliced onion
   and chopped garlic. Sauté,
   covered, over a fairly low heat
   for 20 minutes. Stir once in a
   while with a wooden spoon.

2 Uncover the pot, raise the heat a
   little and add the sugar. Cook for
   10 minutes, stirring now and
   then. (The idea is not to let the
   sugar burn, just to caramelize it
   to give the soup a rich colour.)

3 Sprinkle the flour over the
   onions. Stir it around well.

4 Add the stock to the pot, also the
   wine, thyme and bayleaf. Bring to
   boil, skimming off any scum that
   rises to the surface. Partially
   cover and simmer for 30
   minutes.

5 Just before serving, add the
   sherry.

The garnish
Cut the bread into 2 ½-cm (1-in)
thick slices and toast them on a
baking tray in a warm oven
(165°C 325°F Gas 3) for about 30
minutes, until they are completely
dry. If desired, rub them with a
cut clove of garlic after 15
minutes.

Place a piece of toast on to each
bowl of soup. Sprinkle some
grated cheese on top of each and
place bowls under the grill for a
few minutes to brown the cheese
slightly.

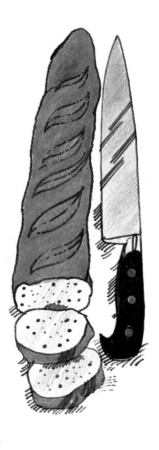

Note Onion Soup can be made
ahead and frozen up to stage 4.

skim off scum

Butter

sliced onion
chopped garlic

Sugar

Flour

thyme

bayleaf

STOCK

White Wine

Sher[ry]

SOUPE À L'OIGNON GRATINÉE

The French Onion Seller

Onion Soup is generally considered French, though why exactly is uncertain. Every country has some form of onion soup, not too different one from another. This heartwarming juicy soup has enjoyed centuries of popularity. Maybe your appreciation will more than equal Monsieur Bovary's, who, in Gustave Flaubert's *Madame Bovary,* returns home to find that 'For dinner there was onion soup . . . and rubbed his hands together in satisfaction and said cheerfully, "It is good to be home again!" '

2 tablespoons oil
¾ kg (1–2 lb) lamb for boiling (some nice bones
included) in one piece
3 litres (5 pints) beef stock _or_ bouillon
1 large onion, chopped
3 medium carrots, chopped
2 stalks celery, chopped
40g (1½ oz) butter
1 teaspoon dried thyme
1 bayleaf
50g (2 oz) pearl barley
100g (4 oz) fresh or frozen peas
salt and pepper to taste

Serves 8–10

1 Heat the oil in a large soup pot and brown the meat in it on all sides. When nicely browned, pour on the stock or bouillon. Bring the mixture to boil.

2 Meanwhile, sauté the onion, carrots and celery in the butter for 5–8 minutes. Add them to the soup pot.

3 Also add the thyme, bayleaf and barley. Simmer, partially covered, for 1½ hours.

4 10 minutes before the end of cooking time, add the peas. Remove the meat, and when cool enough to handle cut off the bone, fat and gristle and discard. Return any lean meat, chopped into small pieces, to the soup.

5 Season to taste with salt and pepper.

Note Scotch Broth reheats and freezes very well.

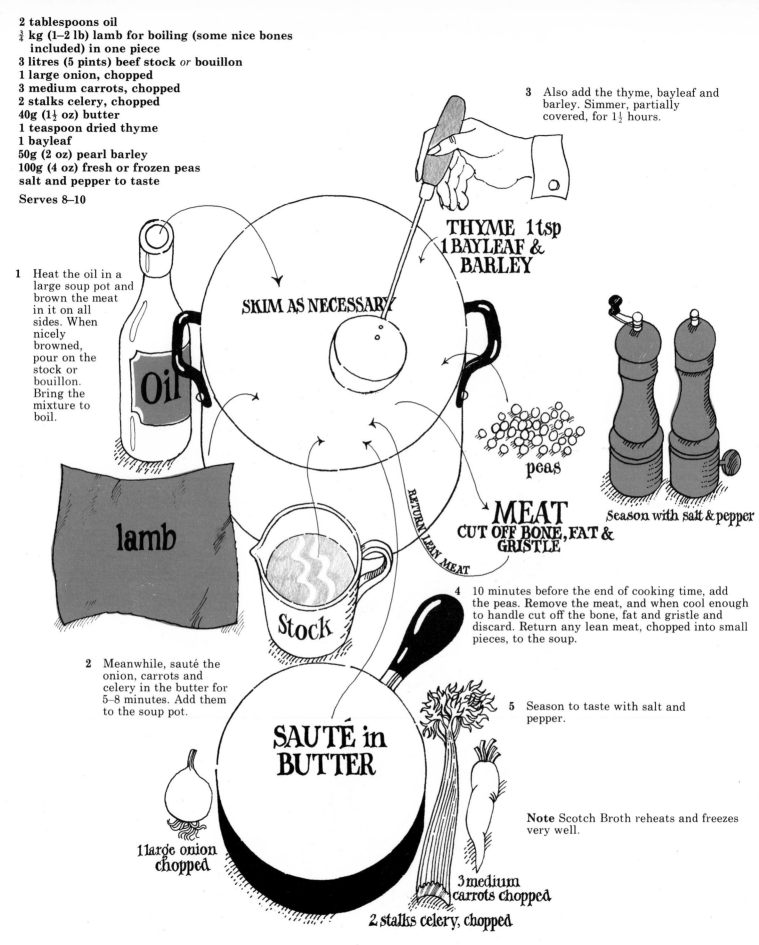

SKIM AS NECESSARY

THYME 1 tsp
1 BAYLEAF &
BARLEY

Oil

peas

lamb

Stock

RETURN LEAN MEAT

MEAT
CUT OFF BONE, FAT &
GRISTLE

Season with salt & pepper

SAUTÉ in
BUTTER

1 large onion
chopped

3 medium
carrots chopped

2 stalks celery, chopped

SCOTCH BROTH

A beautiful soup, hearty, hale and healthy with its origins in simple country fare. Dr Johnson gave recognition to the dish on his tour of Scotland in 1773. Try it on a cold, frosty day, in front of the fire.

500–750g (1–1½ lb) smoked pork hocks *or*
   a ham bone with some meat
2¾ litres (4½ pints) cold water
1 medium carrot, finely chopped
1 medium onion, finely chopped
40g (1½ oz) butter *or* margarine
450g (1 lb) dried split green peas
salt, pepper and nutmeg to taste
chicken stock *or* bouillon as needed
                                    Serves 6

SMOKED PORK HOCKS

SKIM OFF THE SCUM

1 Place the meat in a large pot and add the cold water. Bring to boil, cover and simmer until the meat is tender (2 hours for pork hocks, 1 hour for ham bone).

WATER

2 Meanwhile, sauté the carrot and onion in the butter for 5 minutes.

BUTTER

finely chopped

finely chopped

3 When the meat is tender, add the vegetables to the soup pot. Also add the washed peas. Simmer the soup, uncovered, for 20–30 minutes or until the peas are tender. Skim the soup several times if necessary.

4 Remove the meat from the pot and leave to cool a little. Then cut any lean meat off the bone and cut it into tiny shreds. Discard bone, fat and gristle.

SMOKED PORK HOCKS

5 Purée the soup in a blender, first on low speed then on high until the soup is absolutely smooth.

6 Return the soup to soup pot. Bring back to boil and simmer a few more minutes. Skim off the scum as it appears. Add the meat.

7 If the soup is too thick at this point, thin it down with chicken stock or bouillon to the desired consistency.

Season to taste with salt, pepper and nutmeg.

Note Excellent reheated, and freezes well.

Variations: Instead of the split green peas use: 450g (1 lb) lentils; 450g (1 lb) kidney beans; 450g (1 lb) black beans (soak these overnight); 450g (1 lb) navy beans; 450g (1 lb) split yellow peas; or 450g (1 lb) dried lima beans.

ERWTENSOEP

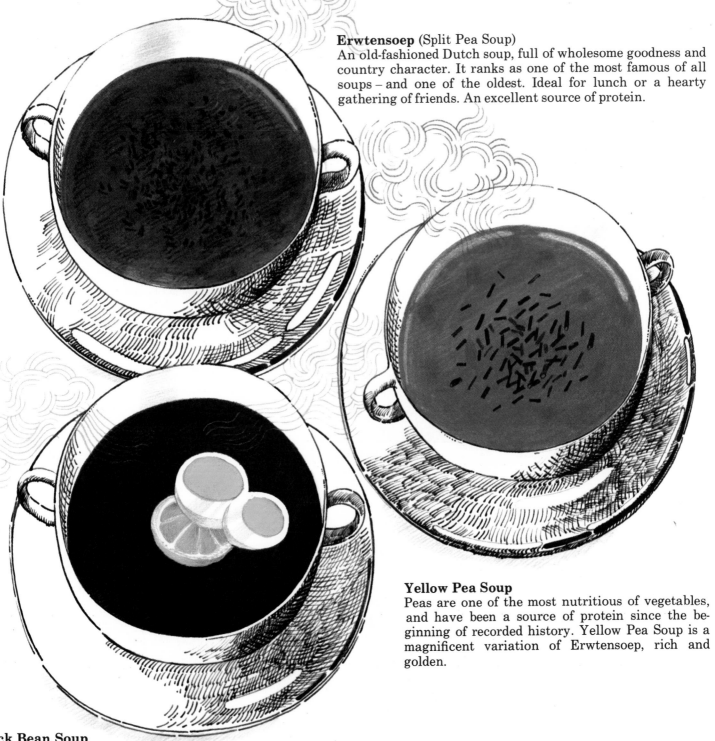

Erwtensoep (Split Pea Soup)
An old-fashioned Dutch soup, full of wholesome goodness and country character. It ranks as one of the most famous of all soups – and one of the oldest. Ideal for lunch or a hearty gathering of friends. An excellent source of protein.

Yellow Pea Soup
Peas are one of the most nutritious of vegetables, and have been a source of protein since the beginning of recorded history. Yellow Pea Soup is a magnificent variation of Erwtensoep, rich and golden.

Black Bean Soup
Black beans are cultivated in the southern United States. They make an especially rich and excellent soup, typical of the south. Beans historically have played an important role in man's diet. 'Full of beans' was an apt and colourful way of describing the state of health and natural good spirits derived from eating beans.
Garnishes for Black Bean Soup are traditionally hardboiled-egg slices and lemon.

39

2 tablespoons oil
3 large onions, roughly chopped
1–3 cloves garlic, crushed (optional)
3–4 level tablespoons paprika
2 tablespoons oil
750g (1½ lb) lean braising (chuck) steak,
    cut into 2½-cm (1-in) cubes
3 medium carrots, chopped
450g (1 lb) tomatoes, skinned and
    roughly chopped *or* equivalent weight
    tinned tomatoes with their liquid
1¼ litres (2 pints) beef stock *or* bouillon
2 large potatoes, cubed
½ teaspoon caraway seeds
½ teaspoon dried marjoram
1 bayleaf
salt and pepper to taste
chopped parsley for garnish
                    Serves 4–5

1   In a large saucepan sauté the
    onion in the oil until soft and
    transparent. Add the garlic, if
    used, and sauté 1 minute longer.

2   Off the heat (when the bubbling
    has subsided), add the paprika.
    Stir until all the onions are
    coated with it. Set aside.

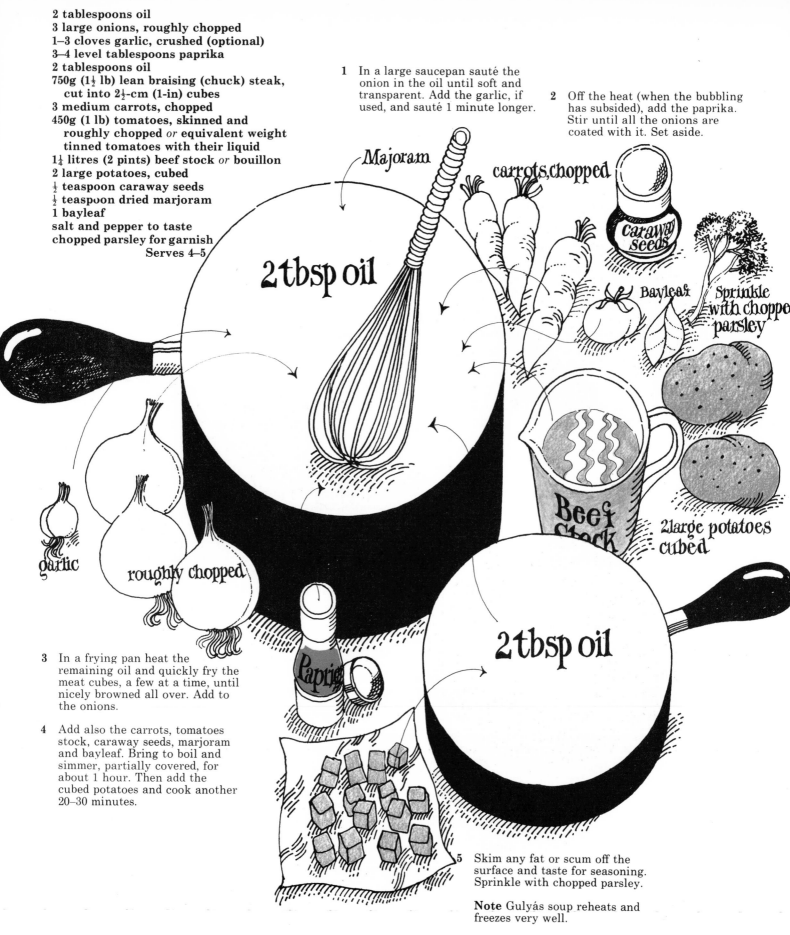

Majoram

carrots, chopped

caraway seeds

2 tbsp oil

Bayleaf

Sprinkle with chopped parsley

Beef Stock

2 large potatoes cubed

garlic

roughly chopped

Paprika

2 tbsp oil

3   In a frying pan heat the
    remaining oil and quickly fry the
    meat cubes, a few at a time, until
    nicely browned all over. Add to
    the onions.

4   Add also the carrots, tomatoes
    stock, caraway seeds, marjoram
    and bayleaf. Bring to boil and
    simmer, partially covered, for
    about 1 hour. Then add the
    cubed potatoes and cook another
    20–30 minutes.

5   Skim any fat or scum off the
    surface and taste for seasoning.
    Sprinkle with chopped parsley.

Note Gulyás soup reheats and
freezes very well.

HUNGARIAN GULYÁS SOUP

Hungary is famous for its many versions of Gulyás, all hearty, down-to-earth country stews that echo the flavour of Hungarian life. Gulyás soup is born of simple peasant fare, and probably evolved as the Magyar tribes roamed central Europe several centuries ago. This soup you will find as colourful and as appetizing to the palate as it is to the eye. Great with a little gypsy music.

2 half chicken breasts
3 litres (5 pints) chicken stock *or*
  bouillon
1 large onion, finely chopped
2 medium carrots, finely chopped
2 stalks celery (with leaves if
  possible), finely chopped
1 bayleaf

40–50g (1½–2 oz) butter *or*
  margarine
3 tablespoons flour
1–2 tablespoons curry powder
75g (3 oz) long grain rice, cooked
salt and pepper
chopped parsley for garnish

Serves 8

1 Place the chicken breasts and the
   stock or bouillon in a large soup pot.
   Bring to boil and simmer *very* gently,
   partially covered, until chicken
   breasts are tender (about 20
   minutes). Remove chicken breasts
   and when cool enough to handle,
   skin and bone them. Cut the
   meat into tiny shreds and set
   aside. Leave the cooking liquid
   in the soup pot.

3 Sprinkle the vegetables with the flour and
   curry powder. Stir well with a wooden spoon
   until all the vegetables are coated.

   Then, with a wire whisk, stir the vegetables
   into the soup pot. Stir well to dissolve the
   flour and curry. Bring to boil and simmer,
   partially covered, for 30 minutes.

Cooked Rice

SALT & PEPPER
CHOPPED PARSLEY
CHICKEN
BREASTS

CHICKEN
Remove & bone

chicken stock

STOCK

4 Add the prepared chicken meat and cooked
   rice and simmer 1 minute longer.

2 In a frying pan sauté the onion, carrots and celery
   in the butter for 5 minutes. Then add the bayleaf.

chopped finely

butter

Flour

CURRY POWDER

BAY LEAF

Season to taste with salt and pepper. Garnish with
chopped parsley.
Note This soup reheats very well, and even
freezes.

Mulligatawny

A smooth succulent spicy broth. Mulligatawny is a semi-Indian dish, one of many that originated as Dutch, Portuguese, French and English traders ventured to the East. Along with other such curry recipes it found its way to Europe in the 18th century.

1 kg (2 lb) cut-up oxtails
4 tablespoons oil
5 tablespoons flour
2¼ litres (4 pints) beef stock *or* bouillon
1 onion, chopped
2 carrots, chopped
1 stalk celery, chopped
1 bayleaf
1 teaspoon dried thyme *or* marjoram
1 clove garlic, crushed (optional)
1 large potato, cubed
1 tablespoon tomato purée
salt and pepper to taste
25g (1 oz) unsalted butter
2–6 tablespoons dry sherry *or* Madeira (optional)

Serves 8

1 Sauté the oxtails in the oil until nicely browned all over. Remove and drain on paper towels.

2 To the remaining fat add the flour and stir until the flour has acquired a nice rich brown colour. (Stir once in a while, because only the flour on the bottom will colour; it needs 'turning over' to brown the rest.) Slowly add the stock or bouillon, stirring all the time with a wire whisk. Bring to boil, skim off the scum and fat, and add the onion, carrot, celery, bayleaf, thyme or marjoram, garlic, potato and tomato purée, and the oxtails. Simmer the soup, partially covered, for 2–3 hours. Skim again if necessary.

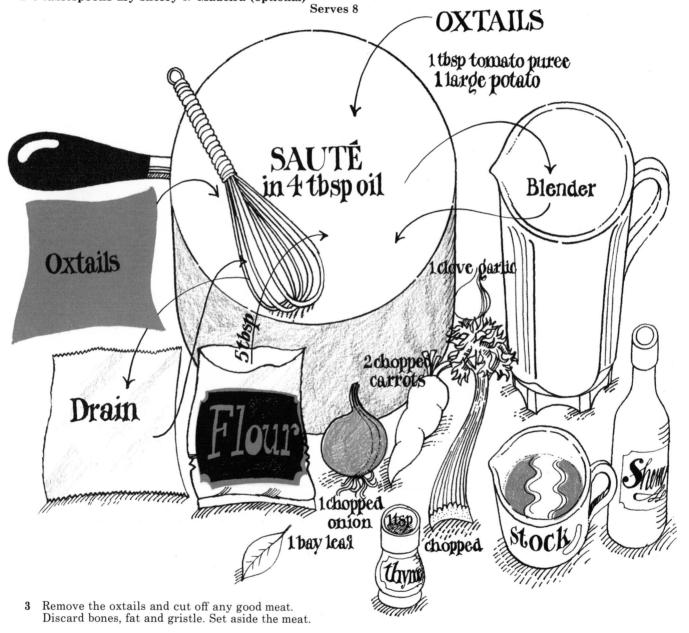

OXTAILS

1 tbsp tomato puree
1 large potato

SAUTÉ in 4 tbsp oil

Blender

Oxtails

Drain

Flour

5 tbsp

1 clove garlic

2 chopped carrots

1 chopped onion

1 bay leaf

1 tsp thyme

chopped

stock

Sherry

3 Remove the oxtails and cut off any good meat. Discard bones, fat and gristle. Set aside the meat.

4 Purée the soup in a blender, return to the soup pot and add the prepared meat to it. Reheat, skimming off any scum and fat that may rise to the surface. Season with salt and pepper.

5 Off the heat, and only just before serving, stir in the soft, unsalted butter and the sherry or Madeira.

Note Can be made ahead or frozen up to stage 4.

44

Oxtail Soup

It is a little difficult to pinpoint the origins of Oxtail Soup. Certainly the ox was one of the earliest of all domesticated animals and as such became part of the human diet. The meat of the ox has been used in many ways, one such being soup, as this Chinese poem, dated 3rd century BC, suggests:

'Ribs of the fatted ox cooked tender and succulent,
        sour and bitter blended in the soup of Wu.'*

This soup is delicious, and overdoing the sherry won't hurt a bit!

*(Birch & Keene, *Anthology of Chinese Literature*)

75g (3 oz) butter *or* margarine
450g (1 lb) fresh okra, sliced *or* 500g
   (1 lb 2 oz) frozen okra, sliced
1 large onion, chopped
1 green pepper, chopped
1 clove garlic, crushed
2 tablespoons flour
generous litre (2 pints) chicken stock
   or bouillon
4 tomatoes, skinned, seeded and
   chopped *or* 450g (1 lb) tinned
   tomatoes, well drained and chopped

2 parsley sprigs } tied together
1 bayleaf
½ teaspoon dried thyme
salt and pepper to taste
3 or 4 half chicken breasts
2 tablespoons Worcestershire sauce
chopped parsley for garnish

Serves 8

optional:
100g (4 oz) cooked hot rice
100 ml (4 fl oz) double cream

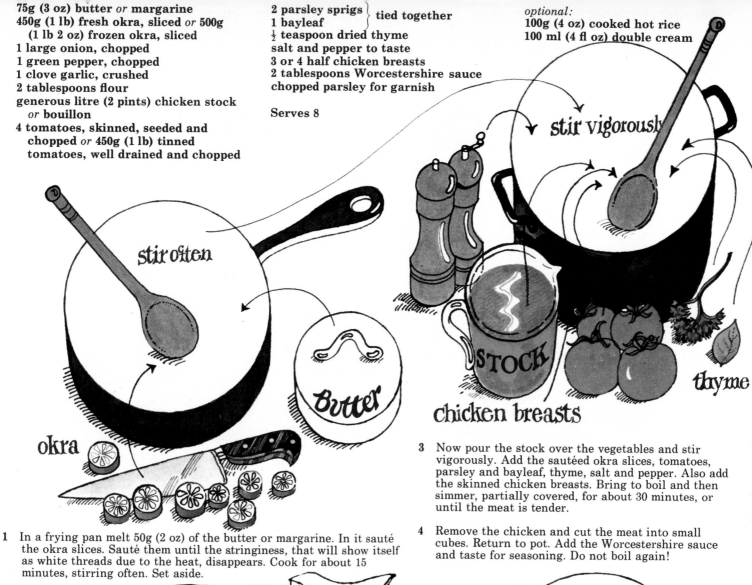

1 In a frying pan melt 50g (2 oz) of the butter or margarine. In it sauté the okra slices. Sauté them until the stringiness, that will show itself as white threads due to the heat, disappears. Cook for about 15 minutes, stirring often. Set aside.

2 In a soup pot melt the remaining butter and sauté the onion and pepper for 5 minutes. Add the garlic and sauté 1 minute. Sprinkle flour over the vegetables. Stir until it has been absorbed.

3 Now pour the stock over the vegetables and stir vigorously. Add the sautéed okra slices, tomatoes, parsley and bayleaf, thyme, salt and pepper. Also add the skinned chicken breasts. Bring to boil and then simmer, partially covered, for about 30 minutes, or until the meat is tender.

4 Remove the chicken and cut the meat into small cubes. Return to pot. Add the Worcestershire sauce and taste for seasoning. Do not boil again!

5 Add the cream, if used. If desired, place a tablespoon of hot rice into each soup plate and ladle the soup over it. Sprinkle with parsley.

Note This soup reheats and freezes well.

SOUTHERN CHICKEN GUMBO

chop
chop
chop

1 onion

4 tomatoes
1 pepper

bouillon

Chicken Stock

1 clove garlic

Okra

3 half chicken breasts

bay leaf

2 sprigs parsley

thyme

Gumbos (poultry, meat, fish or shellfish) are typical of Creole cooking, with okra added to give the soup its glutinous quality. Fresh okra can be bought in Indian communities.

Bon Appetit

750g (1½ lb) soup beef with bone *or* **1 chicken weighing 1½ kg (2–3 lb)**
1¼ litres (2 pints) cold water
1 teaspoon salt
½ teaspoon pepper
1 large stalk celery, roughly chopped
1 large carrot, roughly chopped
1 large onion, roughly chopped
2 parsley sprigs
1 bayleaf
½ teaspoon dried marjoram
25g (1 oz) cooked alphabet noodles
finely chopped parsley for garnish

Serves 4

1 Place the soup beef (or chicken) in a large saucepan. Add the cold water, salt, pepper, celery, carrot, onion, parsley sprig, bayleaf and marjoram. Bring to boil and skim if necessary. Simmer the soup, partially covered, 2 hours for beef, 1 hour for chicken. Remove meat.

2 Strain the soup through a fine-mesh strainer. Discard all the vegetables. Return broth to pot.

3 Cut any lean meat off the soup beef, discarding any bone or fat. If chicken is used, remove one chicken breast, skin and bone it and cut into tiny shreds. Set aside.

4 Put the meat shreds into the broth in the pot. Also add the cooked noodles and the chopped parsley. Cover and leave to stand 2 minutes before serving.

Note This soup can be made ahead a day or two, up to stage 3. If it is to be frozen, put the meat shreds into the broth. Complete stage 4 after defrosting.

For an absolutely clear broth, leave the soup to go cold after stage 3. Whisk 2 egg whites just to break them up, and pour them into the soup. Bring to boil, then simmer, uncovered, for 5 minutes. *Do not stir!* Strain through a fine-mesh strainer lined with a damp cloth.
For garnishes, see Consomme, page 30.

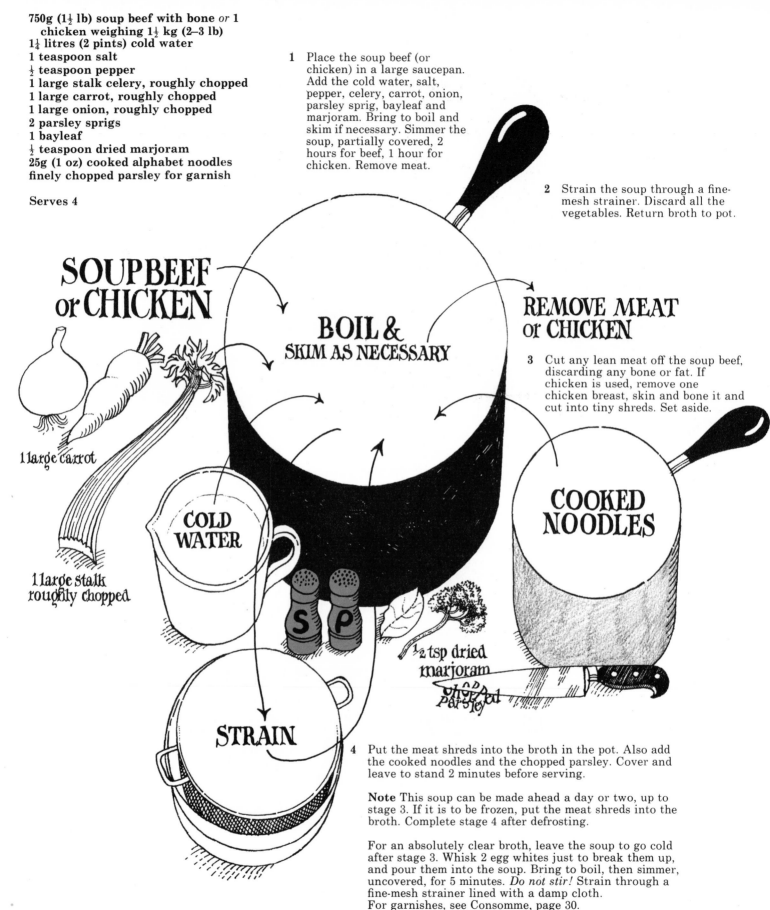

SOUPBEEF or CHICKEN

1 large carrot

1 large stalk roughly chopped

BOIL & SKIM AS NECESSARY

COLD WATER

REMOVE MEAT or CHICKEN

COOKED NOODLES

½ tsp dried marjoram

chopped parsley

STRAIN

FLEISCHBRÜHE

This is an old German soup that has been a hot favourite with countless generations of children. Since its ingredients consist of simple country fare this recipe, or a variation, would almost certainly have been popular when Dr Hoffmann wrote his classic children's story *Struwwelpeter* in 1844, from which 'The Story of Augustus who would not have any soup' is taken. It is a poem that testified to the importance soup played in a child's diet. Though it is difficult to imagine that this particular soup would have been rejected by Augustus. Ever!

This old recipe remains very easy to prepare, is full of nutrition and is a firm favourite with our own children and their friends.

Augustus was a chubby lad;
Fat ruddy cheeks Augustus had.
And everybody saw with joy
The plump & hearty, healthy boy.
He ate & drank as he was told,
And never let his soup get cold.
But one day, one cold winter's day,
He screamed out 'Take the soup away!
O take the nasty soup away!
I wont have any soup today.'

Next day, now look the picture shows
How lean & lank Augustus grows!
Yet, though he feels so weak & ill,
The naughty fellow cries out still
'Not any soup for me, I say,
O take the nasty soup away!
I wont have any soup today.'

The third day comes: Oh what a sin!
To make himself so pale & thin.
Yet when the soup is put on the table,
He screams as loud as he is able,
'Not any soup for me, I say,
O take the nasty soup away!
I wont have any soup today.'

Look at him, now the fourth day's come!
He scarcely weighs a sugar plum;
He's like a little bit of thread,
And, on the fifth day, he was—dead!

1 packet chicken noodle soup mix
2 ripe avocados
juice of ½ lemon (for dipping)
½ small onion, very finely chopped
250 ml (½ pint) single cream
lemon wedges for garnish
chopped chives for garnish (optional)
little salt and pepper if necessary

Serves 4–5

1 Cook the soup mix according to directions. Leave to cool.

3 Put the cold soup, avocados and onion into a blender. Blend on low speed for 1 minute then turn to high and purée the mixture until it is thick and really smooth.

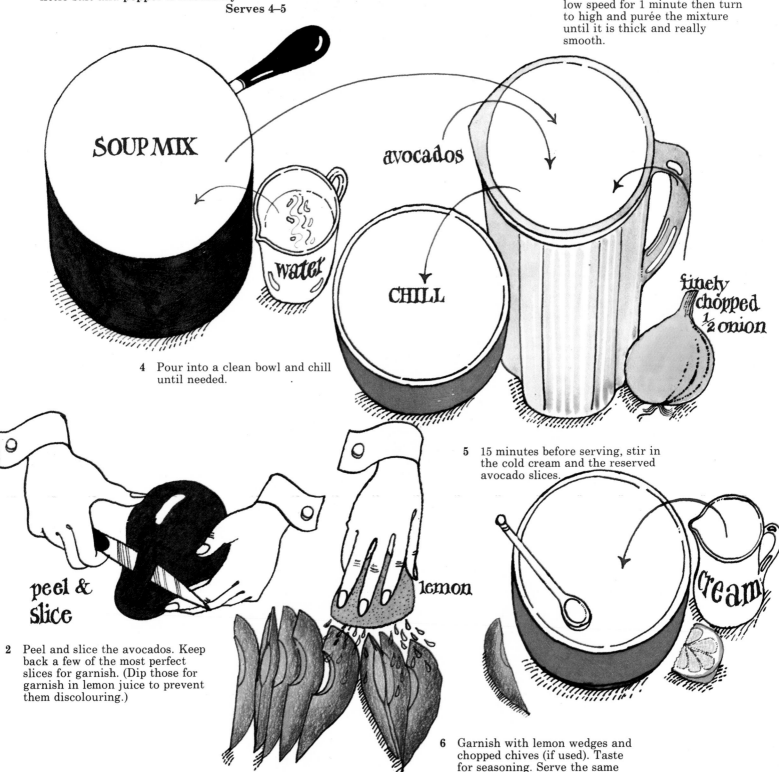

SOUP MIX

water

avocados

CHILL

finely chopped ½ onion

4 Pour into a clean bowl and chill until needed.

peel & slice

lemon

cream

5 15 minutes before serving, stir in the cold cream and the reserved avocado slices.

2 Peel and slice the avocados. Keep back a few of the most perfect slices for garnish. (Dip those for garnish in lemon juice to prevent them discolouring.)

6 Garnish with lemon wedges and chopped chives (if used). Taste for seasoning. Serve the same day!

Note Up to stage 4 the soup can be made 2 hours in advance. Do not freeze!

CALIFORNIAN AVOCADO SOUP

A very delicate soup, cool and refined. Ideal for a hot summer's day when it makes a superb start to a meal. Surprise and delight your friends with its extraordinary subtle taste. Escoffier once said 'Of all the items on the menu, soup is that which exacts the most delicate perfection and the strictest attention.' This soup will stand the closest scrutiny and leave a lasting impression.

1 piece lean boiling beef weighing ¾-1 kg (1½-2 lb)
scant 2 litres (3 pints) beef stock *or* bouillon
1 marrow bone (optional)
450g (1 lb) tinned tomatoes and their juice, chopped
1 stalk celery with leaves, cut into julienne strips
2 stalks parsley ⎫
2 bayleaves   ⎬ tied together
10 peppercorns   ⎭
450g (1 lb) green cabbage, shredded
2 medium onions, chopped

2 medium carrots, cut into julienne strips
1 teaspoon dried dill
¼ teaspoon caraway seeds
100 ml (4 fl oz) red wine (optional)
2 tablespoons vinegar
1 teaspoon sugar
450g (1 lb) cooked beetroot, fresh *or* tinned (including
   juice), cut into julienne strips
100 ml (4 fl oz) sour cream   Serves 5–6

1   Place the meat (and bone, if used) into a large pot. Cover
    with stock and bring to boil over a high heat. Skim off any
    scum that rises to the surface. Simmer the meat, partially
    covered, for about 1 hour. Remove the bone and discard.

BEEF

Stock

REMOVE MEAT
& cut into neat cubes

SKIM AS NECESSARY

**BEETROOT &
JUICE**

1stalk

tom

2 stalks
parsley

2 bayleaves

10 peppercorns

cabbage
shredded

2 medium onions
chopped

2 tbsp vinegar
1 tsp sugar

2 medium
carrots

Dill

Win

¼ tsp caraway

1 tsp

3   Remove the meat and when cool
    enough to handle, cut into neat
    cubes. Discard any fat or gristle.
    Put the meat back into the soup
    pot. This time also add the beetroot
    and juice and simmer another 2
    minutes. Skim if necessary.

Serve the sour cream separately.

2   Add to the soup pot the tomatoes,
    celery, parsley, bayleaves,
    peppercorns, cabbage, carrots,
    onions, dill, caraway, wine, vinegar
    and sugar. Bring back to boil and
    simmer, partially covered, until the
    vegetables are tender (30–40
    minutes).

Note Borscht improves when
reheated. It can also be frozen.

PEPPERCORNS

Dill

SOUR CREAM

Caraway

RUSSIAN BORSCHT

RUSSIAN BORSCHT

Borscht is Russia's most famous main-dish soup. Full of robust goodness, with an unusual flavour. The addition of beetroot gives it a gloriously red colour which contrasts beautifully with the traditional garnish of sour cream.

for the dough
225g (8 oz) plain flour
2 large eggs
1 teaspoon oil
little cold water, if needed
for the filling
**250–275g (10 oz) fresh *or* frozen
   spinach leaves**

450g (1 lb) minced pork
1 teaspoon dried ground ginger
2 spring onions, finely chopped
1 teaspoon oil
3 teaspoons soy sauce
salt and pepper to taste
little dry sherry (optional)
for the soup
**1¾ litres (3 pints) hot, well-flavoured
   chicken stock (not bouillon)**
little chopped parsley for garnish
Serves 6–8

1 Cook the spinach in salted water till tender. Drain. Pick out a few leaves for garnish and set aside. Put the rest back in the pot, and over a medium heat dry them until all the water has evaporated. Chop finely.

3 Mix together the spinach, pork, ginger, spring onions, oil, soy sauce, salt, pepper and sherry (if used). Mix till well blended.

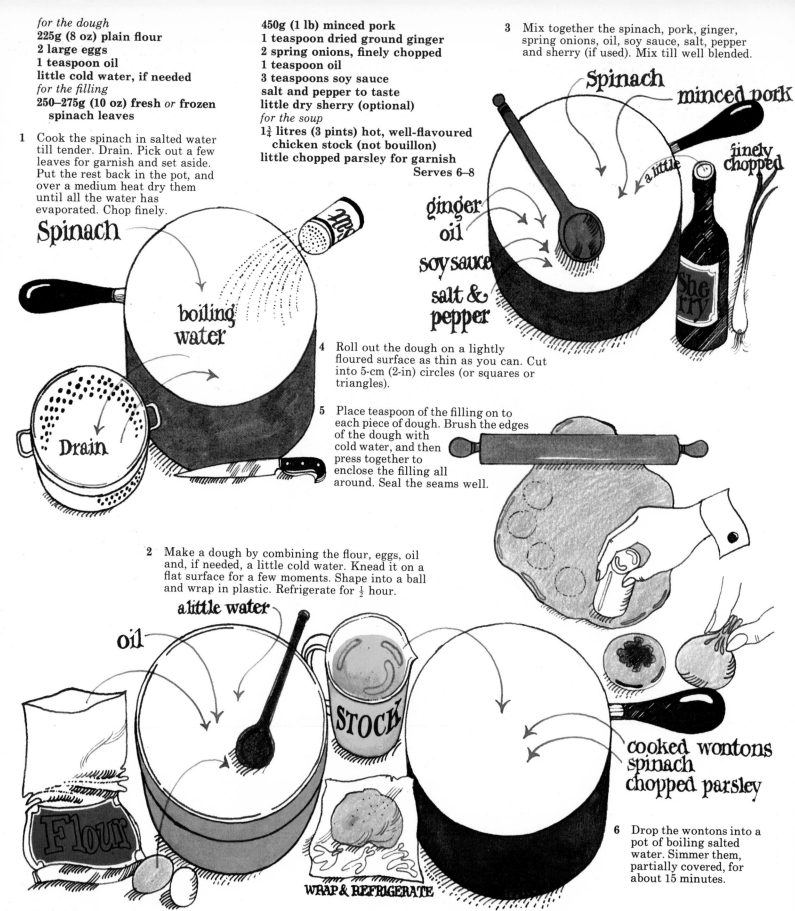

4 Roll out the dough on a lightly floured surface as thin as you can. Cut into 5-cm (2-in) circles (or squares or triangles).

5 Place teaspoon of the filling on to each piece of dough. Brush the edges of the dough with cold water, and then press together to enclose the filling all around. Seal the seams well.

2 Make a dough by combining the flour, eggs, oil and, if needed, a little cold water. Knead it on a flat surface for a few moments. Shape into a ball and wrap in plastic. Refrigerate for ½ hour.

6 Drop the wontons into a pot of boiling salted water. Simmer them, partially covered, for about 15 minutes.

7 Meanwhile, heat the chicken stock and transfer the cooked wontons to it with a slotted spoon. Also add the spinach leaves.

8 Sprinkle with chopped parsley and serve piping hot.

Note Best when fresh. Soup can be reheated if necessary, but do not freeze.

54

CHINESE WONTON SOUP

Wonton Soup is a popular main-dish soup from China. A steaming hot broth, with melt-in-the-mouth dumplings filled with a spicy meat mixture. Truly delightful for an informal dinner party.

1½ kg (2–3 lb) beef flank *or* silverside, tied
securely with string, *or* chuck steak *or*
pot roast
450g (1 lb) chicken backs and necks
3 litres (5 pints) cold water
2 large carrots, chopped
1 medium turnip, chopped
2 leeks, sliced
1 stalk celery, chopped
1 large onion, chopped
2 parsley sprigs ⎫ tied together
1 large bayleaf ⎭
½ teaspoon dried thyme
salt and pepper to taste
1 cut-up marrow bone, tied in a muslin
or cheesecloth bag

Serves 4

1 Place the beef and chicken backs and necks in a heavy pot. Pour over the cold water. Bring to boil over a medium heat. As the scum appears, skim it off and keep skimming for several minutes until the surface is clear. Now add the vegetables and the bundle of parsley and bayleaf, the thyme and some salt and pepper.

2 Partially cover the pot and simmer the soup over the lowest possible heat. Do not let it bubble at all at the sides; cook it really gently! Simmer for 3 hours.

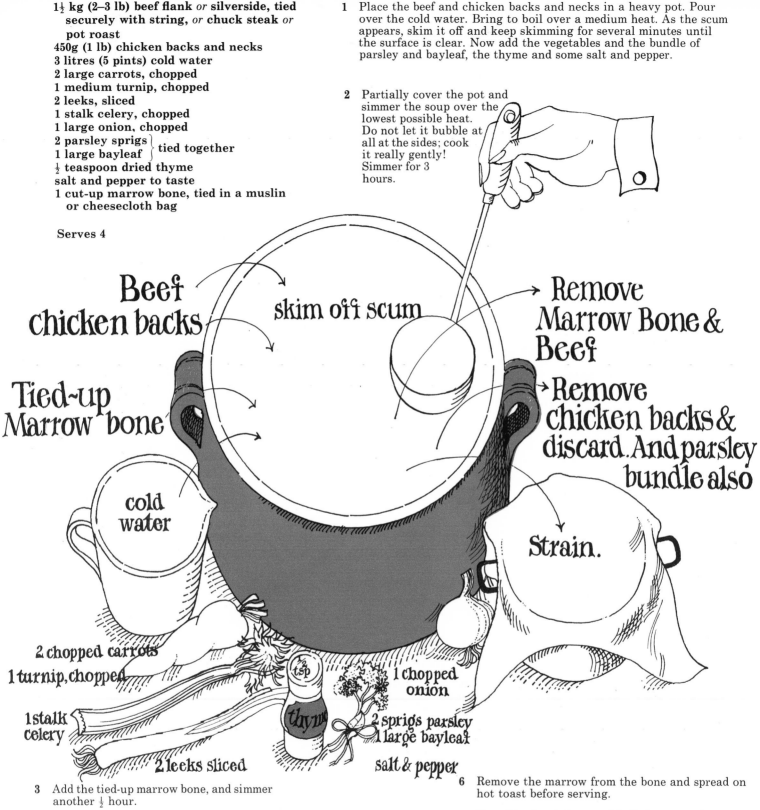

Beef
chicken backs

skim off scum

Remove
Marrow Bone &
Beef

Tied-up
Marrow bone

Remove
chicken backs &
discard. And parsley
bundle also

cold
water

Strain.

2 chopped carrots
1 turnip, chopped
1 stalk celery
2 leeks sliced
tsp
thyme
1 chopped onion
2 sprigs parsley
1 large bayleaf
salt & pepper

3 Add the tied-up marrow bone, and simmer another ½ hour.

4 Remove marrow bone and beef and set aside. Remove chicken backs and necks and parsley bundle, and discard.

5 Strain the broth through a fine-mesh strainer lined with a damp cloth and discard all the vegetables. Taste the broth for seasoning and degrease as much as you can.

6 Remove the marrow from the bone and spread on hot toast before serving.

Note The broth is served ladled over croûtons (see Bouillabaisse, page 14) in shallow soup plates. (Or use any of the garnishes for clear soups, see Consommé, page 30.)
The beef is served carved as a second course, and is traditionally eaten with boiled potatoes and cabbage. Add some garnish, like pickled gherkins, coarse salt, mustard, horseradish or tomato sauce. Reheats well, and any leftover broth can be frozen!

POT·AU·FEU

An extremely old French peasant soup of which there are several regional variations. This classic Pot-au-Feu is made of beef and chicken. In some regions of France it is customary to add veal, pork and sometimes mutton.

Like the stockpot, Pot-au-Feu evolved from the cauldron into which all manner of ingredients were tossed every day. The pot was hung over a fire that was never put out, thus providing an ever-changing broth.

750g (1½ lb) firm fresh red cherries
4 whole cloves
1 cinnamon stick *or* **½ teaspoon ground**
  cinnamon
juice of 1 lemon
1 piece of lemon rind
4 tablespoons sugar
generous 500 ml (1 pint) cold water
25g (1 oz) cornflour
1 glass port *or* **burgundy**   **Serves 4**

4 Crack the cherry stones with a sharp blow of a hammer and place them in a small saucepan. Add the port or burgundy, bring to boil – then remove from heat, cover and leave to infuse for 15–20 minutes. Strain through a fine-mesh strainer and set aside the liquid. Discard stones.

1 Put the cherries, cloves, cinnamon, lemon juice and lemon rind, sugar and water into a soup pot. Bring to boil and simmer, partially covered, until the cherries are tender (15–25 minutes).

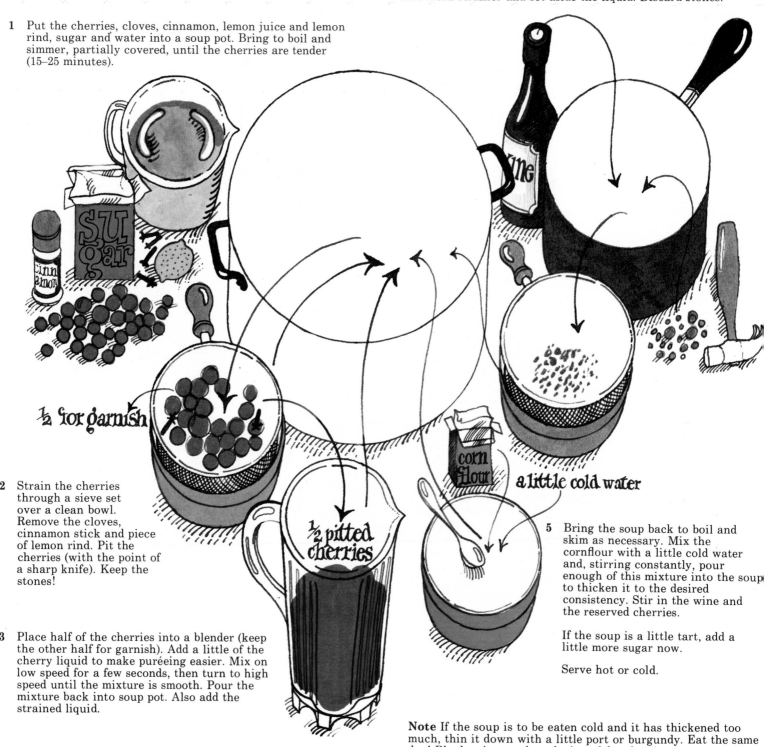

½ for garnish

½ pitted cherries

corn flour

a little cold water

2 Strain the cherries through a sieve set over a clean bowl. Remove the cloves, cinnamon stick and piece of lemon rind. Pit the cherries (with the point of a sharp knife). Keep the stones!

3 Place half of the cherries into a blender (keep the other half for garnish). Add a little of the cherry liquid to make puréeing easier. Mix on low speed for a few seconds, then turn to high speed until the mixture is smooth. Pour the mixture back into soup pot. Also add the strained liquid.

5 Bring the soup back to boil and skim as necessary. Mix the cornflour with a little cold water and, stirring constantly, pour enough of this mixture into the soup to thicken it to the desired consistency. Stir in the wine and the reserved cherries.

If the soup is a little tart, add a little more sugar now.

Serve hot or cold.

Note If the soup is to be eaten cold and it has thickened too much, thin it down with a little port or burgundy. Eat the same day! Blueberries can be substituted for cherries.

KIRSCHSUPPE

A magnificent German soup. Absolutely delicious – try this soup when cherries are in season.
It's a special summer flavour typical of German cooking – with a taste you can't afford to miss!

5 tablespoons sugar
1 small piece lemon peel
$\frac{1}{2}$ teaspoon powdered cinnamon
2 cloves
375 ml ($\frac{3}{4}$ pint) milk
375 ml ($\frac{3}{4}$ pint) dark *or* lager beer
40g (1$\frac{1}{2}$ oz) cornflour
125 ml ($\frac{1}{4}$ pint) double cream
1 egg yolk
1 tablespoon brandy (optional)
1 egg white (optional)   Serves 4

1 Place sugar, lemon peel, cinnamon and cloves in heavy saucepan. Pour over the milk and beer. Leave uncovered and bring to boil, stirring a little so as not to burn the sugar.

2 Mix the cornflour with enough water to make a smooth pouring consistency, and pour enough of this into the soup, stirring all the time with a wire whisk, to reach the desired thickness. The soup should be thickened just enough to coat the back of a spoon. Boil for just half a minute. Remove from heat.

LEMON PEEL   5 tbsp

Remove lemon peel & cloves

sugar

$\frac{1}{2}$ tsp

cinnamon

1 egg yolk

Double cream

MILK

BEER

4 tbsp

Water

CORN FLOUR

BEAT EGG WHITE

3 Mix together the cream and egg yolk and, stirring briskly, mix it into the hot soup. Also stir in the brandy (if used).

4 Remove the lemon peel and cloves, and add a little more sugar if desired.

5 Beat the egg white (if used) until stiff and gently fold it into the soup, just enough to break it up a little. Cover the pot and leave the egg white to set 2 minutes before serving. Serve hot or cold, but eat the same day!

Biersuppe

Guten Appetit

Biersuppe is a typically German soup that in all probability dates back several centuries. It is further testimony to the German love of beer. In Germany, it is usually made with dark beer which has a very low alcohol content. Mostly it is eaten hot, usually preceding a cold evening meal. When made with lager beer it is best eaten well chilled.

STOCKS

Beef Stock

2½–3 kg (5–6 lb) beef bones (shin and marrow mixture)
2 pigs feet, split in half
scant 5 litres (8 pints) cold water
225g (8 oz) carrots, chopped
225g (8 oz) onions, chopped
2 stalks celery, chopped
1 bouquet garni, comprising: 2 parsley sprigs } tied together
                                              1 bayleaf
1 teaspoon dried thyme

Place the bones and pigs feet into a large pot. Cover them with cold water.
    Bring the pot to boil over a high heat. As the scum appears on the surface, skim it off see under Skimming. Keep skimming it for about 30 minutes, until the scum ceases to rise. (You don't have to be too careful at this point, most of the liquid being scooped up is water.) Now add the chopped vegetables and the bouquet garni and simmer the stock, only partially covered, for 8 hours.
    Strain the stock through a damp cloth set in a sieve over a large pot or pail. Discard the bones and vegetables.
    Store the stock in individual 500 ml (1-pint) containers. It can be refrigerated for about 2 weeks, or frozen for months.

Chicken Stock

2–2½ kg (4–5 lb) chicken backs and necks
scant 5 litres (8 pints) cold water
225g (8 oz) carrots, chopped
225g (8 oz) onions, chopped
2 stalks celery, chopped
1 bouquet garni, comprising: 2 parsley sprigs } tied together
                                              1 bayleaf
½ teaspoon dried thyme

Place chicken backs and necks into a large pot. Cover them with the cold water.
    Bring to boil. As the scum appears on the surface, skim it off. Keep skimming until the scum no longer appears (see Beef Stock).
    Add the cut-up vegetables and the bouquet garni and simmer, partially covered, for 5 hours.
    Strain and store as for Beef Stock.

Fish Stock

1 medium carrot, chopped
1 medium onion, chopped
1 stalk celery, chopped
1 bayleaf
2 parsley sprigs } tied together
½ teaspoon dried thyme
generous litre (2 pints) cold water
generous litre (2 pints) dry white wine
1½ kg (3 lb) whitefish heads and tails

Place all ingredients in a large pot. Bring to boil. As the scum appears, skim it off very carefully (you don't want to waste any of the wine!). Skim until the scum no longer appears otherwise the stock will be cloudy.
    Simmer the stock, partially covered, for about 1 hour.
    Strain and store as for Beef Stock.

SALAD CONTENTS

INTRODUCTION

The Salad! A bowl of luscious, fresh greens coated with a smooth, subtle dressing, or raw vegetables, marinated and flavoured with a hint of spice or herbs. Such are the mouth-watering delights which can accompany the gourmet meal or family fare alike.

Why then is the salad so neglected, or even absent from the British dinner table? For the British, the salad is usually symbolized by the presence of a few wet lettuce leaves, a slice or two of tomato, some cucumber and a dash of salad cream.

This concept is enough to make many a continental cook cringe. For the continental European, the salad in one form or another is a source of infinite variety, always crisp and fresh, winter and summer alike. It is not as though there is any greater choice or supply of fresh vegetables, simply that the continental palate demands that a salad should give further colour and imagination to a meal, and complement and enhance the taste. Nor do they cling to a basic green salad, but frequently make use of seasonal vegetables.

These pages are an attempt to provide a collection of recipes and ideas which will stimulate the reader to discover the delights of the salad – a delight to the eye as well as the palate. Also, for those people who are already salad devotees, I hope the variety, and especially the inclusion of many less-familiar European salads, will give them renewed interest. I have tried to gather together a greater variety of recipes than is usually found in any one cookbook.

A good salad does not just happen, a lot of love and attention has to go into its preparation. Handle it gently at all times, and you will be rewarded by utmost crispness. The actual tossing of the finally assembled ingredients is, for most people, quite a ritual – something usually done at the dinner table, with infinite care being taken not to bruise a single leaf.

Creating a salad is truly underrated, for it can be a source of great joy. The pure tenderness of fresh greens serves to stimulate and refresh the palate, so that what accompanies or follows can be more fully appreciated. Nothing can match natural foods eaten when they are at their best, and most nutritious. Typical are the very humble, yet versatile Green Salad – a classic recipe – or Chef's Salad from America. In fact all the salads in the book are classics of one kind or another, all from different parts of the world, all with their own individual tastes and characteristics.

I have tried to give emphasis to the use and suitability of certain vegetables at certain times of the year. Seasonal vegetables are at their best and cheapest when fresh. This is an added bonus, but by no means a prerequisite to the preparation of a fine salad.

Finally, whatever your motivation for discovering the salad, or rediscovering it, I trust that it will add colour, imagination and enjoyment to your cooking and eating. For that is what the delights of the salad are all about.

Bon appétit!

HINTS ON HOW TO MAKE YOUR SALAD A HIT

THE DO'S & DON'TS

Here are some hints on the selection of ingredients and their preparation, which will help you to get the most out of your salad.

Lettuce
Handle it gently at all times! I have been horrified only too often to see a greengrocer stuff a lettuce into too small a paper bag, causing it to bruise. Bruises are waste – especially with Round and Cos lettuce, which are especially fragile. Webb and Curly Endive are less so.

Always wash the lettuce well, but make sure it is completely dry before tossing it with vinaigrette dressing because the dressing will not adhere to wet leaves. The best way to do this is to wrap the washed leaves in a towel (or paper towel) and leave them in the refrigerator for 2–3 hours. The towel helps to soak up the water, and the salad will

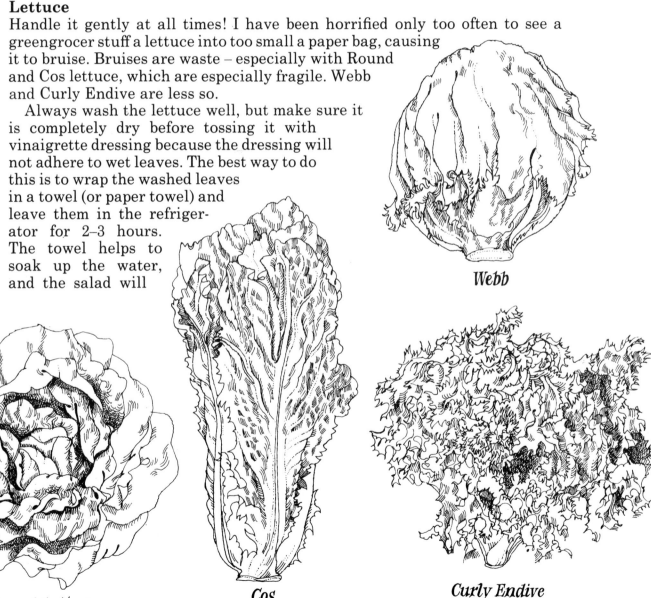

Webb

Round Lettuce

Cos

Curly Endive

The four most popular lettuces in Britain

65

come out crisp and dry. The dark in the refrigerator also helps because light tends to make lettuce leaves wilt more quickly.

Another way to dry lettuce is to shake the washed leaves gently in a wire basket or a colander, but take care not to bruise them.

Never cut lettuce with a knife, always tear it into bite-sized pieces. This gives the leaves a greater absorbency along the tear.

It is best not to toss the salad until just before serving – preferably at the dinner table – because it will go limp quite quickly once it comes into contact with the oil. However, I must admit that I cheat sometimes, when I have a lot of last-minute cooking to do. I make up the dressing in a bowl, pile the dried lettuce leaves loosely on top, and leave it in the refrigerator, covered with a paper towel, for an hour or even longer. Then all I need to do is toss it immediately before serving.

Cucumber

Cucumbers are often bitter at the blossom end. To avoid pulling the bitterness all through the cucumber, make it a habit to cut the cucumber in half first – and peel it from the cut edge to within 13 mm ($\frac{1}{2}$ inch) of the ends. Another point is that cucumbers shed a lot of water when they come into contact with salt, therefore it is advisable to sprinkle the peeled, sliced cucumber with some salt, and leave the slices to drain for at least half an hour in a colander. Then rinse off the salt, making sure the slices are quite dry before mixing them with the dressing.

Garlic

Some people find the use of garlic objectionable, therefore it is listed in most recipes as being optional. When it is not listed as being optional I would suggest that you should use it, for in such cases it is the only way to catch the authentic flavour of these salads.

Ask yourself why it is that you do not like it. Could it be that the smell of garlic follows you around – on your chopping board, your chopping knife, your fingers? If so, try sprinkling some salt on your chopping board, then dip your knife into it. Then cut or crush your garlic clove in the salt. You will not smell a thing!

Sometimes it is enough just to rub a salad bowl with a cut clove of garlic; this way you do not actually eat it. Another way to give a salad a slight garlic flavour is the French way of rubbing a piece of stale bread with a cut clove of garlic and then tossing it around with the greens and the dressing. Remove the bread before serving the salad. This piece of bread is known as a *chapon*.

Oil

Most cookbooks will have you believe that only olive oil will do. Authentic vinaigrette dressing does indeed call for olive oil, but in fact any oil found on your supermarket shelf can be used. You might even prefer it to olive oil, which is very heavy. Only in recipes where I specifically recommend olive oil would I urge you to use it for maximum authenticity.

Vinegar

The same applies to vinegar. Red or white wine vinegars are undoubtedly more delicious, but try buying the unflavoured ones. Then you can add your own flavourings, either herbs from your garden or dried ones from your kitchen shelf. This brings more variety into your dressings. Ordinary vinegars are also most enjoyable though, and certainly much cheaper, and added herbs give them quite a unique flavour. You will find that I have mostly used ordinary vinegars in my recipes.

Instead of vinegar you can use an equal quantity of fresh lemon juice. This can make a very pleasant change. If the lemon dressing seems a little sour, add a sprinkle of sugar to it.

Salad Bowls

The ideal salad bowl for tossed salads is a large wooden one, with a large wooden spoon and fork. The softness of the wood is least likely to bruise the salad. They should be washed quickly (never soaked) in warm soapy water and dried straight away.

Glass bowls are also very attractive, as are china or ceramic ones. Just make sure they are not made of a porous material, in other words, they must be well glazed. Naturally you would not let vinegar touch silver or metal bowls.

Salad Dressings

For tossed green or mixed salads only a vinaigrette dressing (oil, vinegar or lemon) is acceptable. I tend to have a personal dislike for all the creamy concoctions in bottles and jars. I find home-made ones acceptable, though only on Webb lettuce, since this is the only kind of lettuce that does not collapse under a heavy dressing. A salad is designed to stimulate the palate, but a salad with a creamy dressing tends to have the reverse effect. However, for those who cannot live without creamy dressings I have given recipes for some of the more popular ones.

As regards mayonnaise, I would like to stress that you should only use a good commercial one, or, better still, make your own.

Never, never use any kind of commercial salad cream for any of the recipes in this book.

When and How to Serve

Salads can start a meal and be served as an hors d'oeuvre, or go with a meal and accompany the main dish, or come after the main course. When eaten before a meal as an hors d'oeuvre, the salad should be served on individual chilled plates, and eaten with just a fork. The same applies to salads eaten after the main course. Salads eaten with the main course are best served on individual plates or small bowls and placed at the top left hand side of the dinner plate. It is also quite acceptable to serve a salad on the same plate as the main course, especially with rice or pasta dishes, when no vegetable is served.

One note of advice: always serve a salad at some point during a dinner party. Your guests will appreciate the fresh, cool change.

Diet conscious or not, a salad can make an ideal meal in itself.

Winter Salads

In the depths of winter, resort to hothouse lettuces, red and green cabbages, Dutch cabbage, potatoes, the occasional cucumber or tomato, and tinned stuffs, such as green beans, or asparagus. Fresh mushrooms are usually available even in mid-winter.

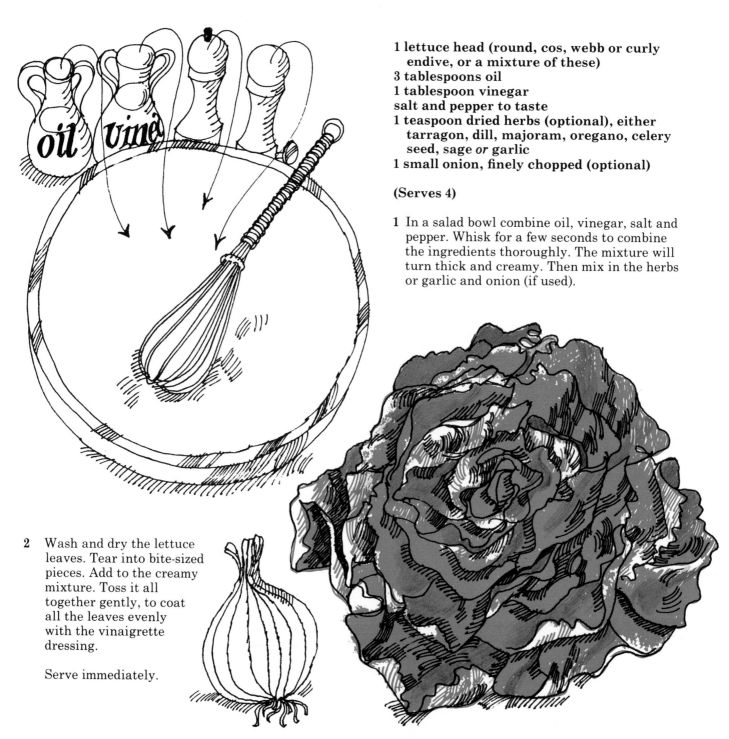

1 lettuce head (round, cos, webb or curly endive, or a mixture of these)
3 tablespoons oil
1 tablespoon vinegar
salt and pepper to taste
1 teaspoon dried herbs (optional), either tarragon, dill, majoram, oregano, celery seed, sage *or* garlic
1 small onion, finely chopped (optional)

(Serves 4)

1 In a salad bowl combine oil, vinegar, salt and pepper. Whisk for a few seconds to combine the ingredients thoroughly. The mixture will turn thick and creamy. Then mix in the herbs or garlic and onion (if used).

2 Wash and dry the lettuce leaves. Tear into bite-sized pieces. Add to the creamy mixture. Toss it all together gently, to coat all the leaves evenly with the vinaigrette dressing.

Serve immediately.

Note:
The Green Salad is also the basis for making a Mixed Salad – simply add your own choice of vegetables (tomato, cucumber, radishes, watercress, mustard cress, red and green peppers, sliced mushrooms, etc.).

The Basic Green Salad

This is probably the world's most popular and versatile salad.
The classic French vinaigrette dressing gives it a tangy kind of
flavour, guaranteed to refresh the palate. As a side dish the green
salad will accompany any main course. It is a must with all rice and
pasta dishes.

When you are unsure which vegetable to have with a certain dish,
the green salad will always prove an excellent choice.

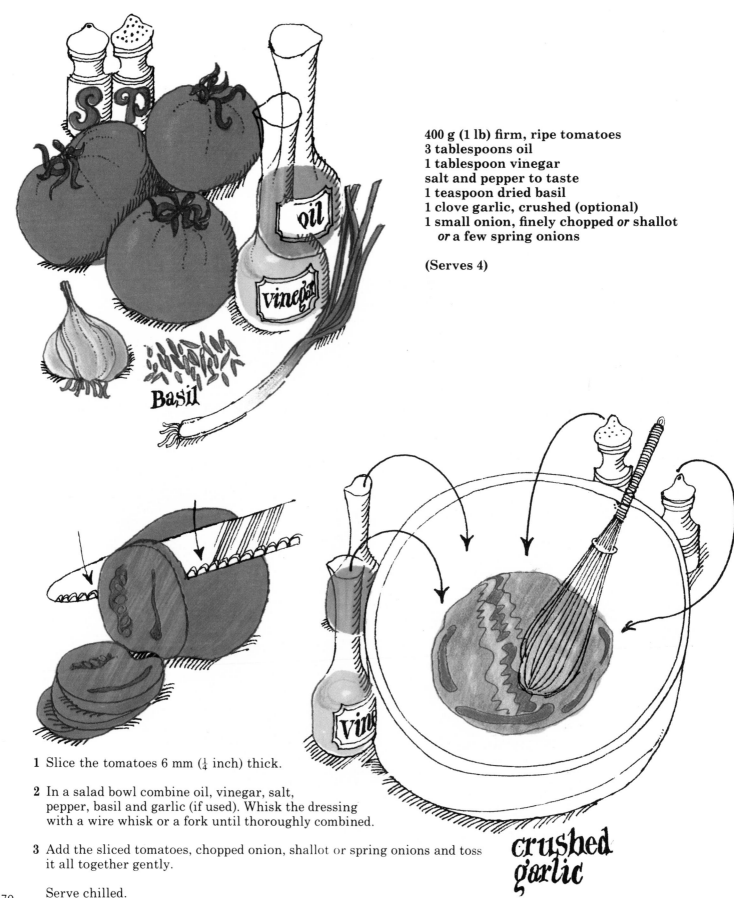

400 g (1 lb) firm, ripe tomatoes
3 tablespoons oil
1 tablespoon vinegar
salt and pepper to taste
1 teaspoon dried basil
1 clove garlic, crushed (optional)
1 small onion, finely chopped *or* shallot
   or a few spring onions

(Serves 4)

1 Slice the tomatoes 6 mm (¼ inch) thick.

2 In a salad bowl combine oil, vinegar, salt,
pepper, basil and garlic (if used). Whisk the dressing
with a wire whisk or a fork until thoroughly combined.

3 Add the sliced tomatoes, chopped onion, shallot or spring onions and toss
it all together gently.

Serve chilled.

TOMATO SALAD

Especially fine in summer, when tomatoes are at their peak. Cool and
juicy, it is ideal for serving with fried dishes – particularly steak, chops or fish.
A bowl of tomato salad will add a brilliant splash of colour to the dinner table.
A touch of basil, together with the garlic, highlights the authentic
continental flavour of this recipe.

1 cucumber
2 tablespoons oil
2 tablespoons vinegar
salt and pepper to taste
¼ teaspoon dried dill
3–4 spring onions, chopped *or* **1 small onion, chopped**
1 tablespoon double cream *or* **evaporated milk**

(Serves 4)

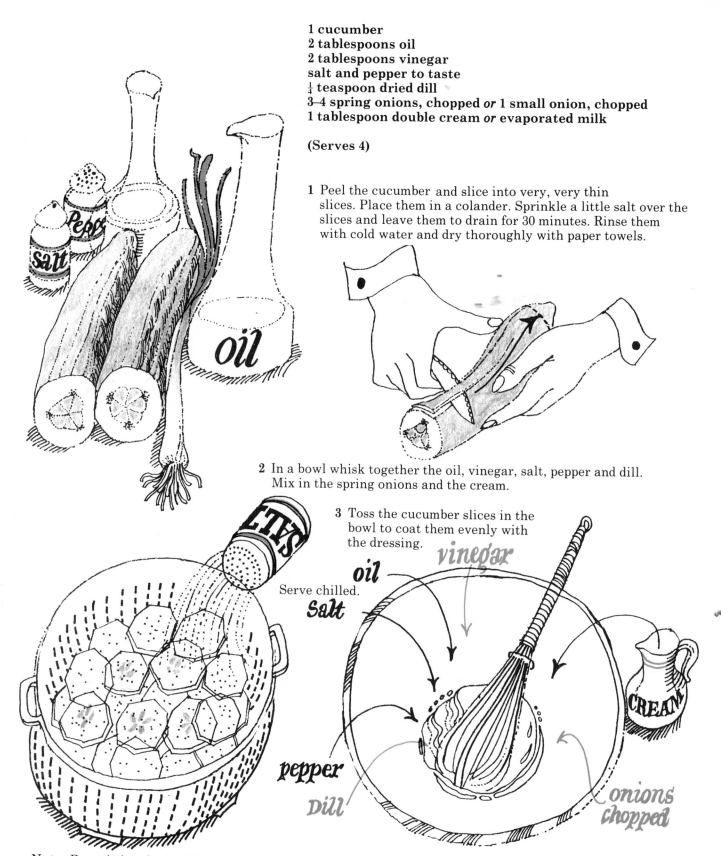

1 Peel the cucumber and slice into very, very thin slices. Place them in a colander. Sprinkle a little salt over the slices and leave them to drain for 30 minutes. Rinse them with cold water and dry thoroughly with paper towels.

2 In a bowl whisk together the oil, vinegar, salt, pepper and dill. Mix in the spring onions and the cream.

3 Toss the cucumber slices in the bowl to coat them evenly with the dressing.

Serve chilled.

Note: By omitting the draining procedure (preparing the dressing first and then slicing the peeled cucumber into it) the dressing will be diluted by the juice from the cucumber. This also makes a delicious salad, and children love the juice.

CUCUMBER SALAD

This beautifully juicy salad with a taste of spring is very smooth on the palate, and is ideal with rice dishes or new, buttered potatoes. The addition of dill gives it a slightly sweet and very delicate taste. A favourite with children.

400 g (1 lb) good, small potatoes
  (They must stay in one piece when
  boiled, new ones are usually the safest.)
2 tablespoons vinegar
½ teaspoon sugar
salt and pepper to taste

1 small onion, finely chopped
1 heaped tablespoon chopped gherkin
  (optional)
3–4 heaped tablespoons good mayonnaise
1 hard-boiled egg, cut into wedges
a little chopped parsley

(Serves 3 or 4)

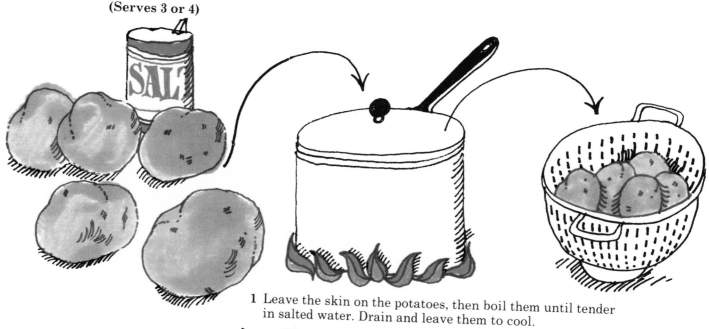

1 Leave the skin on the potatoes, then boil them until tender in salted water. Drain and leave them to cool.

2 Meanwhile, put the vinegar, sugar, salt and pepper into a bowl and whisk to combine. Add chopped onion and gherkin (if used) and the peeled, thinly sliced potatoes. (Halve the larger potatoes to keep all the slices small.)

3 Add the mayonnaise, mix it all well and garnish with the hard-boiled egg and chopped parsley

4 Leave to marinate for 1 hour.

Note: This salad will keep for a day or two if kept tightly covered in a refrigerator. To freshen it up again, toss in 1 tablespoon of boiling water before serving.

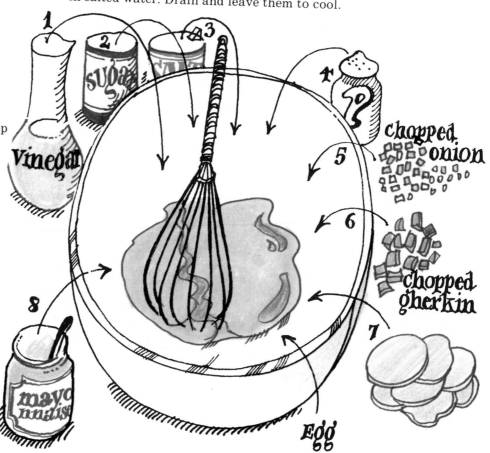

Kartoffel Salat

I always think of this salad as being distinctly German, and
this is an authentic German recipe. The taste is especially fine
with frankfurters, any cold meat, and, would you believe it,
fried fish. You may find it even more to your liking than chips.
In Germany no picnic is complete without the potato salad.

1 small Dutch cabbage, about 400 g (1 lb)
salt and pepper to taste
½ teaspoon sugar
2 tablespoons vinegar
1 small green pepper, deseeded and sliced (optional)
1 teaspoon celery seed (optional)
3 tablespoons good mayonnaise
chopped chives *or* parsley

(Serves 4–6)

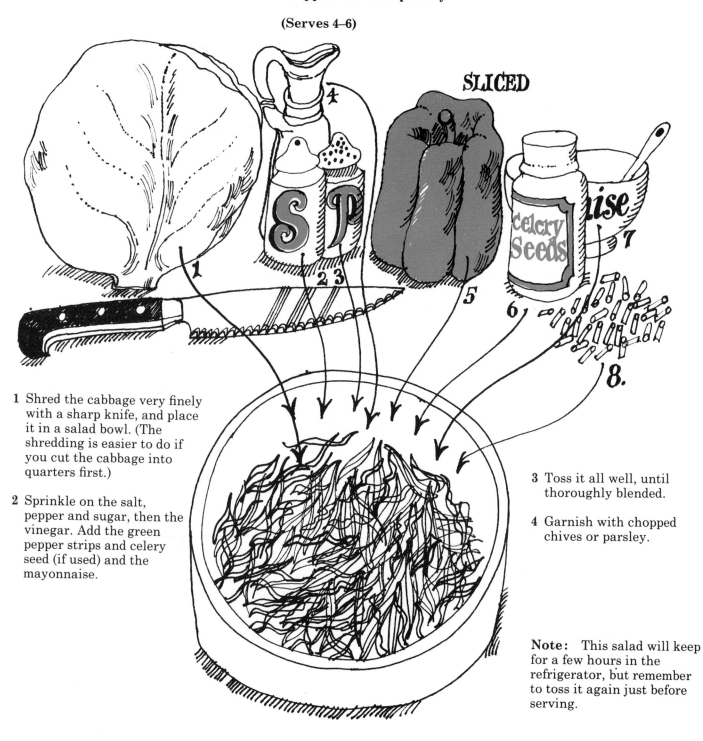

SLICED

1 Shred the cabbage very finely with a sharp knife, and place it in a salad bowl. (The shredding is easier to do if you cut the cabbage into quarters first.)

2 Sprinkle on the salt, pepper and sugar, then the vinegar. Add the green pepper strips and celery seed (if used) and the mayonnaise.

3 Toss it all well, until thoroughly blended.

4 Garnish with chopped chives or parsley.

Note: This salad will keep for a few hours in the refrigerator, but remember to toss it again just before serving.

COLESLAW

Coleslaw is something I have been eating as long as I can remember. It is especially popular on the Continent and in North America. Its creamy dressing makes it ideal as an accompaniment to fish, chips or hamburger, or for that matter, any fried meat.

800 g (2 lbs) cooked beetroot, cut into slices
1 large onion, cut into rings
100 ml (4 fl oz) vinegar
100 ml (4 fl oz) water
1 dessertspoon sugar
1 bayleaf
4 peppercorns
2 whole cloves
½ teaspoon salt
½ teaspoon caraway seeds (optional)

(Serves 4)

1 Cook the beetroot in salted water until tender, peel them and cut them into slices.

2 Place them in a deep, china or glass dish together with the onion rings.

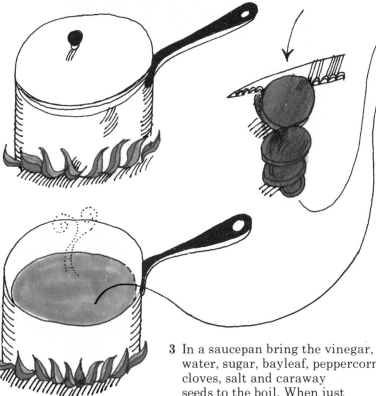

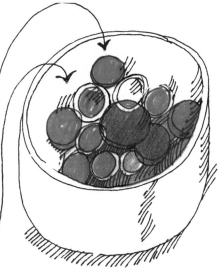

4 Leave to cool and then refrigerate until ready to use.

3 In a saucepan bring the vinegar, water, sugar, bayleaf, peppercorns, cloves, salt and caraway seeds to the boil. When just reaching boiling point, pour this marinade over the beetroot and onions.

Note: This salad will keep for about a week if tightly covered and kept in the refrigerator.

Beetroot Salad

This salad was one of my Grandmother's favourites. The marinade gives it a unique taste and distinctive, old-fashioned kind of flavour. Especially good with cold meats, fried fish and potato dishes. In Britain greengrocers often sell beetroot already boiled, which makes things much easier.

Especially good for weight watchers – almost zero calories.

400 g (1 lb) green string beans *or* 1 large tin cut green beans
3 tablespoons oil
1 tablespoon vinegar
salt and pepper to taste
1 small onion, finely chopped *or* shallot *or* some spring onions
½ teaspoon dried tarragon, oregano, dill or garlic (optional)
1 sprig of parsley for garnish

(Serves 4)

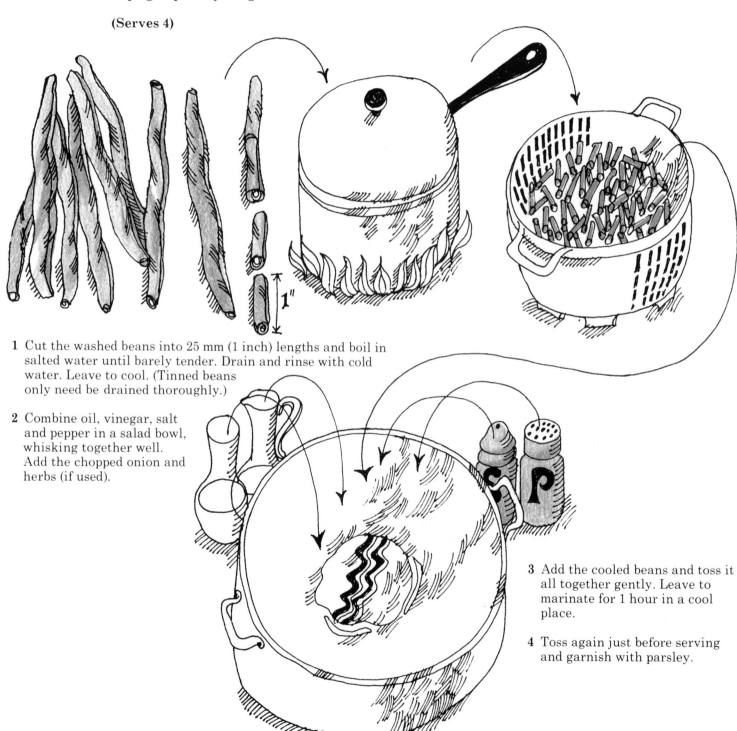

1 Cut the washed beans into 25 mm (1 inch) lengths and boil in salted water until barely tender. Drain and rinse with cold water. Leave to cool. (Tinned beans only need be drained thoroughly.)

2 Combine oil, vinegar, salt and pepper in a salad bowl, whisking together well. Add the chopped onion and herbs (if used).

3 Add the cooled beans and toss it all together gently. Leave to marinate for 1 hour in a cool place.

4 Toss again just before serving and garnish with parsley.

Bohnensalat

An old German salad. This is my own recipe,
inherited from my mother, who inherited it
from her mother, who I suspect inherited it
from her mother. However, this particular version
I like to feel is distinguished by its simplicity.
Smooth and soft, it can be served instead of a vegetable
with just about any dish.

4 firm green peppers
1 clove garlic
¼ teaspoon salt
5 tablespoons olive oil
1 small tin pimientos
   or add 1 red pepper to the green ones
a few stoned black olives

(Serves 4)

1 To skin the peppers spear them on a
  fork and scorch the skin over a flame
  until it turns quite black, then
  scrape it off with a knife.

2 Cut the skinned peppers into
  quarters and remove all the seeds.
  Then cut them into strips.

3 Crush the clove of garlic into the
  salt, until it turns almost to a
  liquid, then with a wire whisk beat
  in the oil in a thin, steady stream.

4 Arrange the peppers attractively on a
  platter, scatter the pimientos (or the red
  pepper strips) over them, and pour the
  dressing over. Garnish with the olives.
  Cover the dish and leave the flavours to
  mingle for 30–60 minutes.

Note: This salad will keep for 2–3 days if
kept tightly covered in a refrigerator.

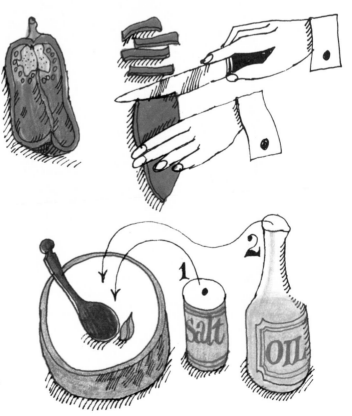

Green Pepper Salad Provençale

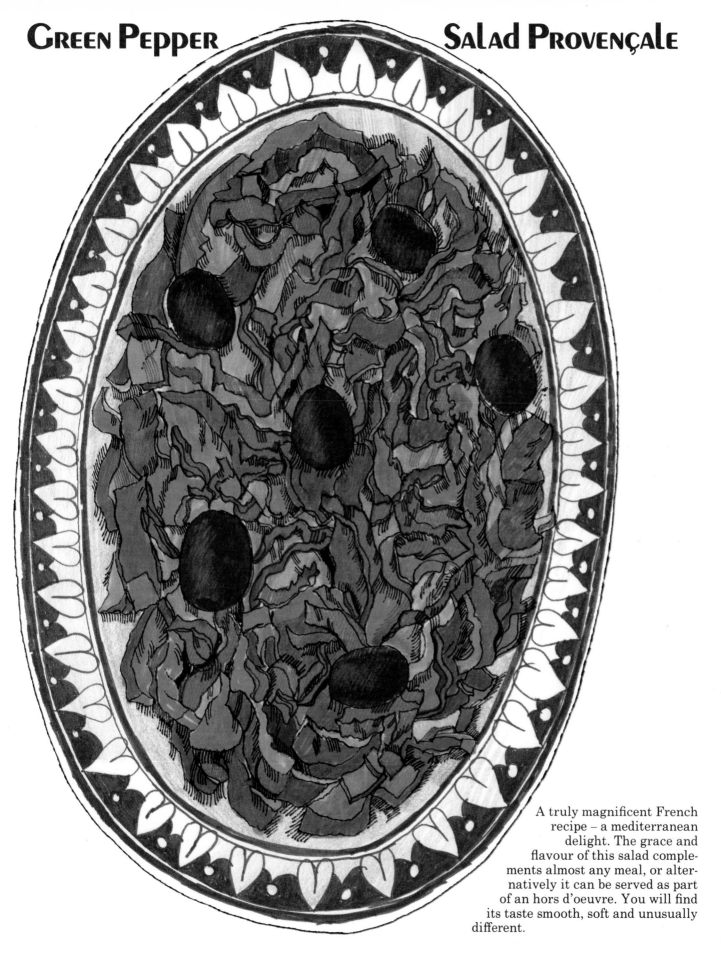

A truly magnificent French recipe – a mediterranean delight. The grace and flavour of this salad complements almost any meal, or alternatively it can be served as part of an hors d'oeuvre. You will find its taste smooth, soft and unusually different.

200 g (½ lb) firm, green or white cabbage, thinly shredded
200 g (½ lb) red cabbage, thinly shredded
salt and pepper to taste
1 green pepper, deseeded and cut into strips (optional)
1 small onion, thinly sliced
4 tablespoons oil
2 tablespoons vinegar
1 tablespoon chopped parsley

(Serves 4–6)

1 Cut both cabbages into quarters and shred them very thinly with a sharp knife. Discard the core.

2 Place the shredded cabbage in a bowl, add the salt, pepper, green pepper strips and onion rings. Toss lightly.

3 In a screwtop jar combine oil and vinegar and shake until thoroughly blended.

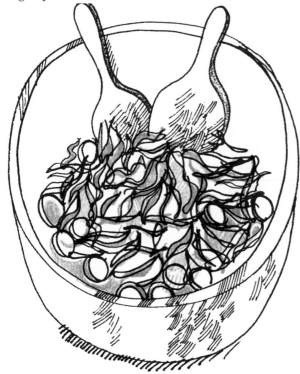

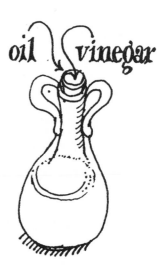

oil vinegar

4 Pour it over the salad, toss it thoroughly and refrigerate until ready to use.

5 Just before serving toss it again lightly and sprinkle with the chopped parsley.

RAW CABBAGE SALAD

An extremely crunchy, tangy and crisp salad, which is highly nutritious, and can be eaten any time of the year. The cabbage salad has a certain earthiness which is always refreshing and stimulating to the palate. It makes a fine winter salad.

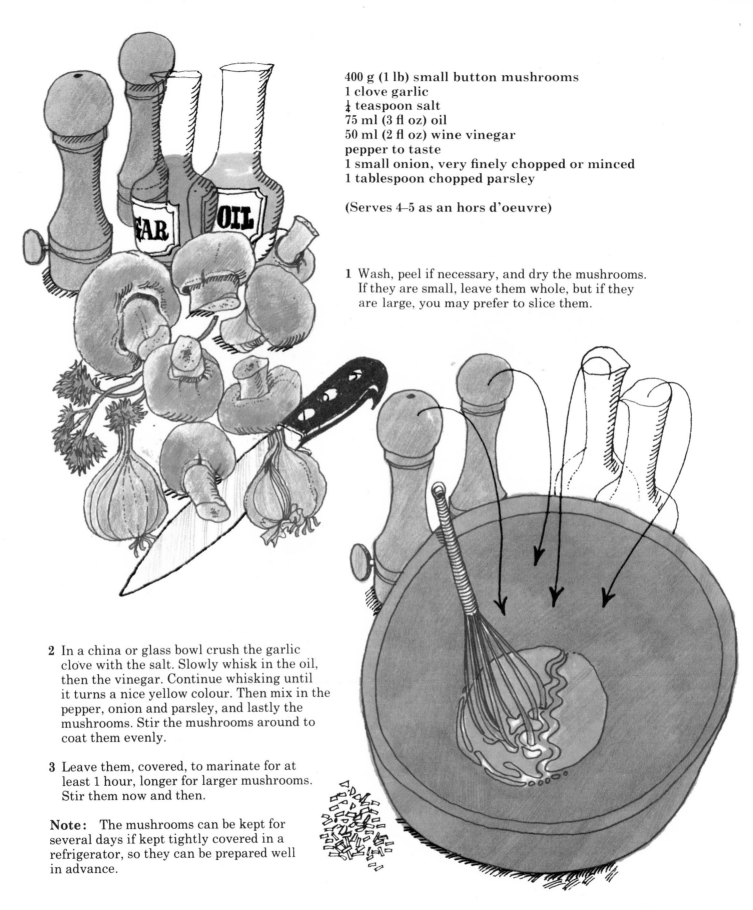

400 g (1 lb) small button mushrooms
1 clove garlic
¼ teaspoon salt
75 ml (3 fl oz) oil
50 ml (2 fl oz) wine vinegar
pepper to taste
1 small onion, very finely chopped or minced
1 tablespoon chopped parsley

(Serves 4–5 as an hors d'oeuvre)

1 Wash, peel if necessary, and dry the mushrooms.
  If they are small, leave them whole, but if they
  are large, you may prefer to slice them.

2 In a china or glass bowl crush the garlic
  clove with the salt. Slowly whisk in the oil,
  then the vinegar. Continue whisking until
  it turns a nice yellow colour. Then mix in the
  pepper, onion and parsley, and lastly the
  mushrooms. Stir the mushrooms around to
  coat them evenly.

3 Leave them, covered, to marinate for at
  least 1 hour, longer for larger mushrooms.
  Stir them now and then.

Note: The mushrooms can be kept for
several days if kept tightly covered in a
refrigerator, so they can be prepared well
in advance.

Mushroom Salad

A magnificent and unusual taste. The marinade 'cooks' the mushrooms to leave them soft and absolutely delicious. Mushroom salad can be served as an hors d'oeuvre, or as part of a buffet.

1 small celeriac
38 g (1½ oz) chopped walnuts
200 g (8 oz) green grapes, pips removed
1 small eating apple
juice of 1 lemon
4 tablespoons good mayonnaise
salt and pepper to taste
chives or parsley, chopped, for garnish

(Serves 4)

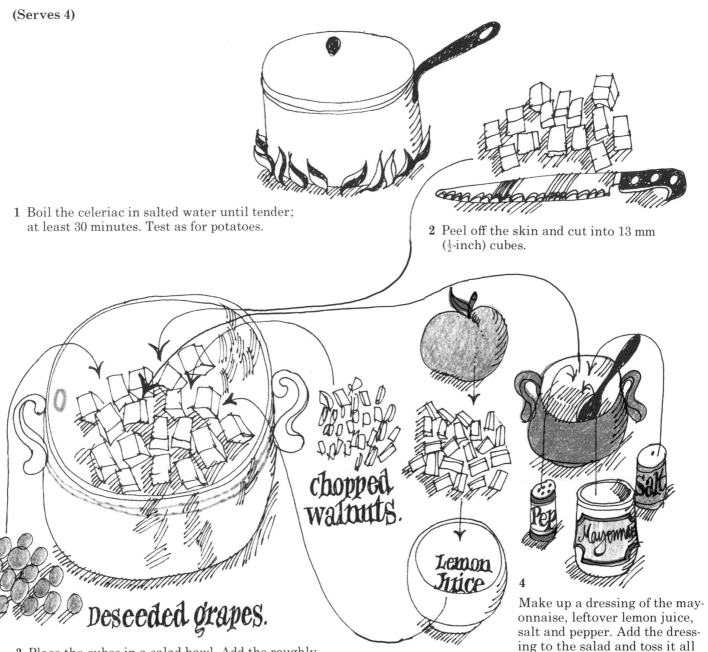

chopped walnuts.

Lemon Juice

Deseeded grapes.

1 Boil the celeriac in salted water until tender;
at least 30 minutes. Test as for potatoes.

2 Peel off the skin and cut into 13 mm
(½-inch) cubes.

3 Place the cubes in a salad bowl. Add the roughly
chopped walnuts and the deseeded grapes. Peel the
apple and cut it into small pieces. Coat the apple
pieces with lemon juice to prevent them discolouring. Add to the salad bowl.

4 Make up a dressing of the mayonnaise, leftover lemon juice,
salt and pepper. Add the dressing to the salad and toss it all
together lightly but thoroughly.

5 Refrigerate until ready to use, then
sprinkle on the chives or parsley.

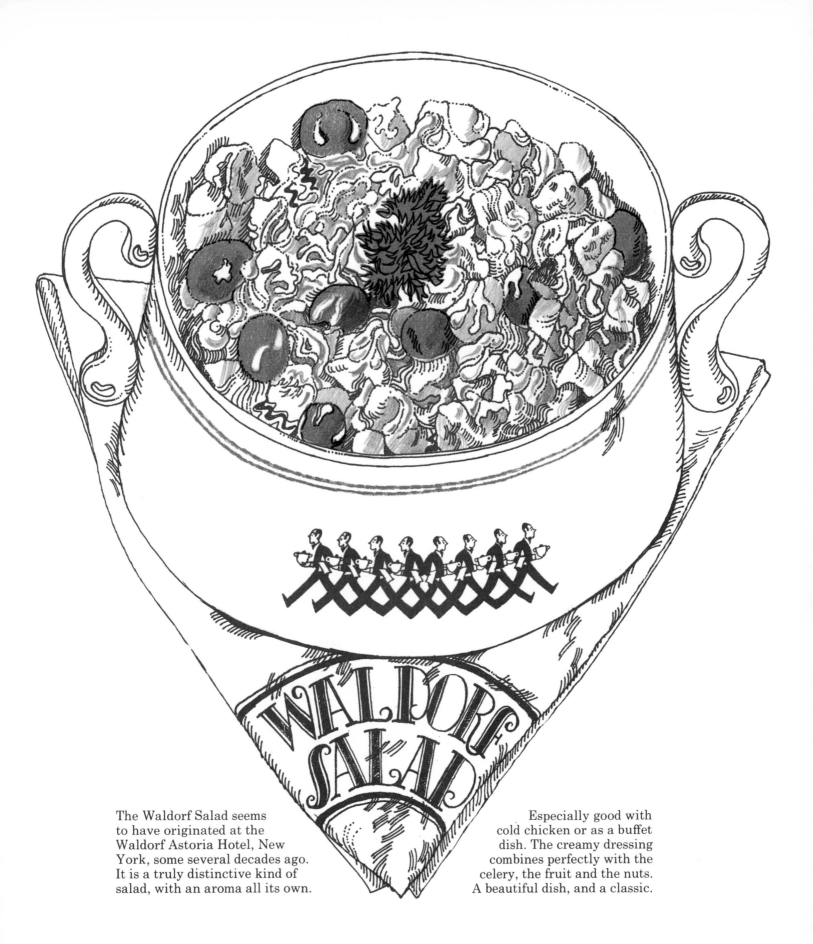

The Waldorf Salad seems to have originated at the Waldorf Astoria Hotel, New York, some several decades ago. It is a truly distinctive kind of salad, with an aroma all its own.

Especially good with cold chicken or as a buffet dish. The creamy dressing combines perfectly with the celery, the fruit and the nuts. A beautiful dish, and a classic.

2 lettuce hearts
2 tins tuna fish
10 or so stoned black olives
1 onion, cut into rings
2 tomatoes, cut into wedges
100 g (4 oz) or more cooked string beans
1 green pepper, cut into strips
1 hard-boiled egg, cut into wedges
100 ml (4 fl oz) olive oil
50 ml (2 fl oz) white wine vinegar
¼ teaspoon dried tarragon
¼ teaspoon dried dill
salt and pepper to taste
1 clove garlic, crushed

(Serves 4 for lunch or 6 as an hors d'oeuvre)

1 Wash and dry the lettuce and tear it into bite-sized pieces. Line a nice platter with it.

2 Mound the tuna fish in the centre and garnish the platter attractively with olives, onion rings, tomatoes, string beans, pepper strips and wedges of hard-boiled egg.

3 Make a vinaigrette dressing from the rest of the ingredients in a screwtop jar or bottle, and shake it to combine it all thoroughly.

4 Pour the dressing over the salad and serve immediately.

Note: Niçoise salad lends itself to great variations. Sometimes it can also include boiled and cubed potato, anchovy fillets, cooked artichoke bottoms or peas.

SALAD NIÇOISE

A French provincial classic, generally accepted as originating in Nice. A truly great salad, which is almost a complete meal in itself.

Its combination of ingredients give it a wholesome country character, ideal for a summer lunch. It can also be served as an hors d'oeuvre.

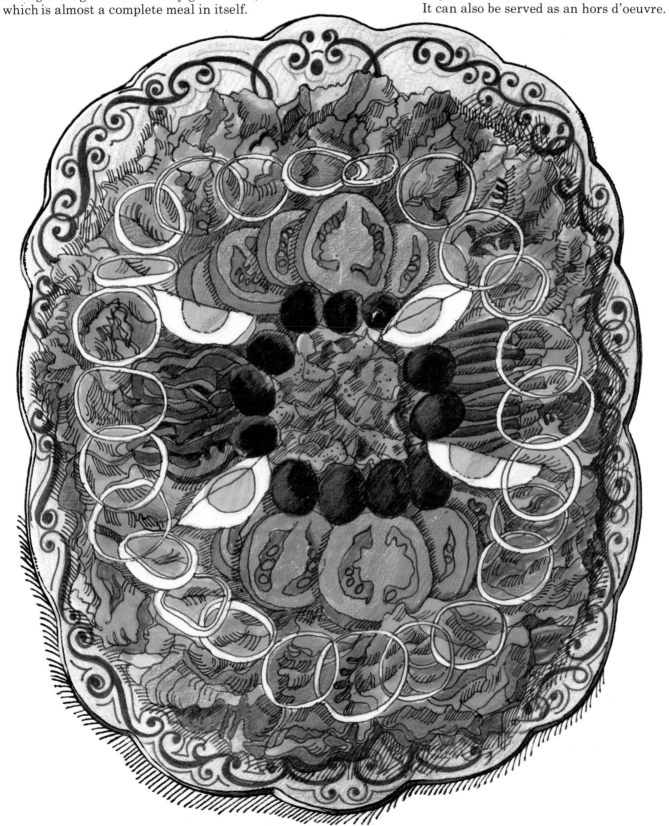

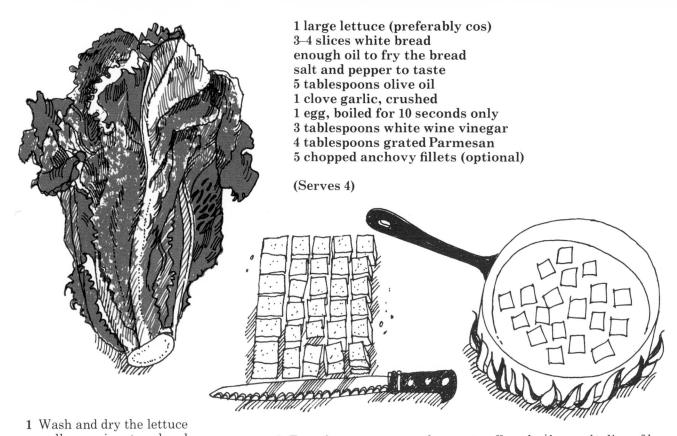

1 large lettuce (preferably cos)
3–4 slices white bread
enough oil to fry the bread
salt and pepper to taste
5 tablespoons olive oil
1 clove garlic, crushed
1 egg, boiled for 10 seconds only
3 tablespoons white wine vinegar
4 tablespoons grated Parmesan
5 chopped anchovy fillets (optional)

(Serves 4)

1 Wash and dry the lettuce well, wrap in a towel and refrigerate until ready to use.

2 To make *croutons*, cut the crusts off, and cube, each slice of bread. Fry the cubes in oil until nicely browned all round.

3 Now tear the lettuce into bite-sized pieces and put into a large salad bowl. Add the salt and pepper and the olive oil and crushed garlic and toss gently.

4 Break the egg over it, add the vinegar and toss again lightly.

5 Sprinkle the Parmesan and anchovy fillets (if used) over it all and toss again lightly.

6 Sprinkle the *croutons* over everything.

Serve immediately.

Caesar Salad

A southern Californian classic. The rich tender
greens make a particularly crisp salad. The fresh
flavour of the dressing make it a highly distinctive
dish for the connoisseur or novice alike. There are
numerous variations of the Caesar Salad, but to the
best of my knowledge this recipe is the most
authentic.

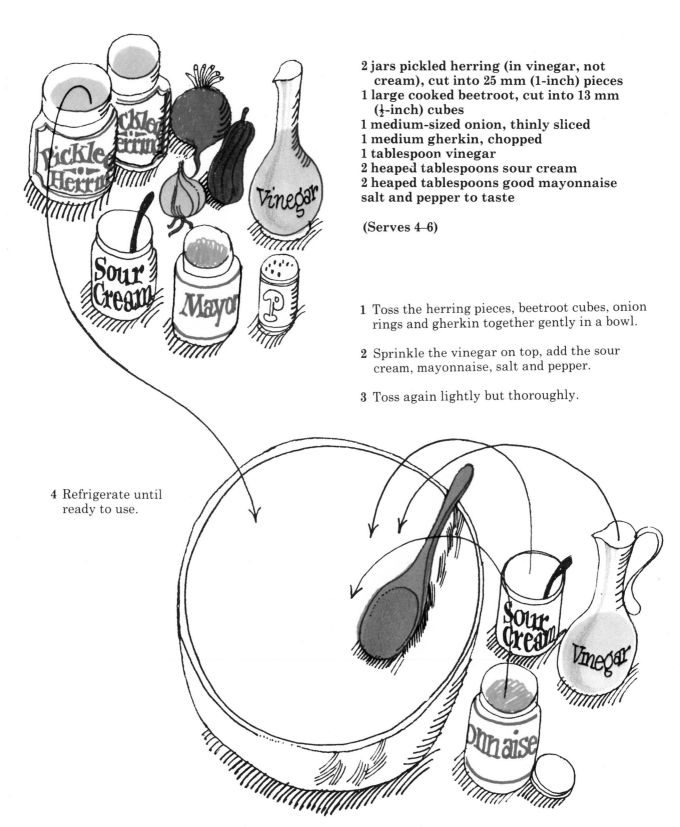

2 jars pickled herring (in vinegar, not
     cream), cut into 25 mm (1-inch) pieces
1 large cooked beetroot, cut into 13 mm
     (½-inch) cubes
1 medium-sized onion, thinly sliced
1 medium gherkin, chopped
1 tablespoon vinegar
2 heaped tablespoons sour cream
2 heaped tablespoons good mayonnaise
salt and pepper to taste

(Serves 4–6)

1 Toss the herring pieces, beetroot cubes, onion
   rings and gherkin together gently in a bowl.

2 Sprinkle the vinegar on top, add the sour
   cream, mayonnaise, salt and pepper.

3 Toss again lightly but thoroughly.

4 Refrigerate until
   ready to use.

Note: This salad will keep for a day or two if tightly covered and kept in a refrigerator.

Hering Salat

A simple version of an authentic German recipe. Creamy,
fishy and beautifully smooth. It makes an ideal hors d'oeuvre
or buffet dish, or, as a midnight snack after a late night
out, it will help to clear your head the morning after.

1 onion, thinly sliced
1 orange, cut into segments
4 tablespoons oil
4 tablespoons vinegar
salt and pepper to taste
1 lettuce head

(Serves 4)

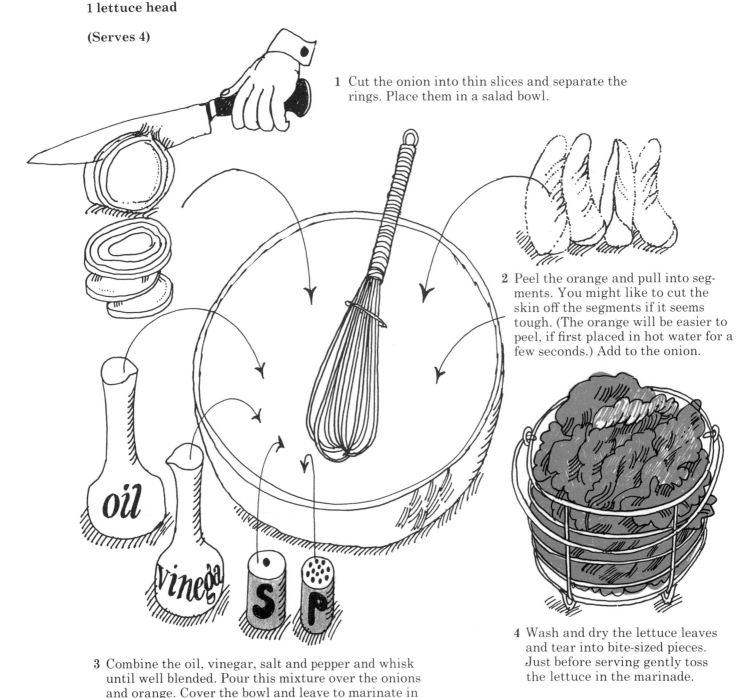

1 Cut the onion into thin slices and separate the rings. Place them in a salad bowl.

2 Peel the orange and pull into segments. You might like to cut the skin off the segments if it seems tough. (The orange will be easier to peel, if first placed in hot water for a few seconds.) Add to the onion.

3 Combine the oil, vinegar, salt and pepper and whisk until well blended. Pour this mixture over the onions and orange. Cover the bowl and leave to marinate in the refrigerator for 1 hour.

4 Wash and dry the lettuce leaves and tear into bite-sized pieces. Just before serving gently toss the lettuce in the marinade.

Serve immediately.

Spanish Salad

The orange and onion give this salad a really delightful flavour. Crisp, juicy and truly refreshing, it is a salad that can be enjoyed at any time of the year.

The combination of flavours goes well with light meat, chicken or fish.

1 lettuce head (preferably Webb)
200 g (8 oz) cold, cooked chicken, cubed
100 g (4 oz) thick sliced ham, cubed
100 g (4 oz) cheese, cubed (any kind)
2 hard-boiled eggs, cut into wedges
2 tomatoes, cut into wedges
1 bunch watercress
5 spring onions
a **Salad Dressing** *or* the
   vinaigrette dressing for Salad Niçoise.

(Serves 4)

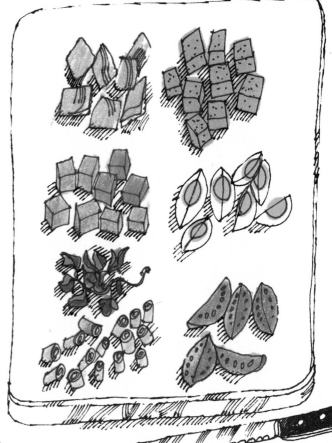

1 Wash and dry all the vegetables. Tear the
lettuce into bite-sized pieces, and place in a
wide, shallow bowl or on a platter.

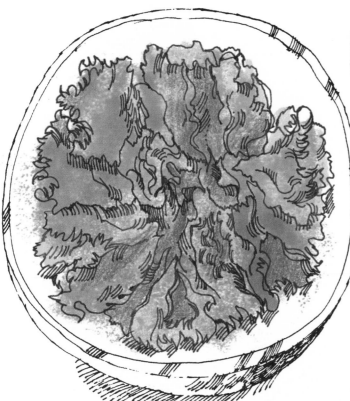

2 On top of the lettuce arrange the chicken
cubes, ham cubes, cheese cubes, egg wedges,
tomato wedges, watercress and spring onions,
in an attractive pattern.

3 Pass the dressing separately in a small bowl.
Let everyone help themselves to the salad
first, and then pour the dressing over to suit
their own taste.

Chef's Salad.

This is generally recognised as an American salad. It makes an ideal light lunch or supper and is refreshing on a hot summer's day. Try it with a glass of wine and a chunk of crusty bread, or as a picnic salad.

enough raw spinach for your needs
1 small cucumber
salt
2 tablespoons red wine vinegar
4 tablespoons oil
pepper to taste
a little dry mustard

(Serves 4)

1 Wash the spinach well and clean off any tough
   leaves and stems. Leave to dry completely.

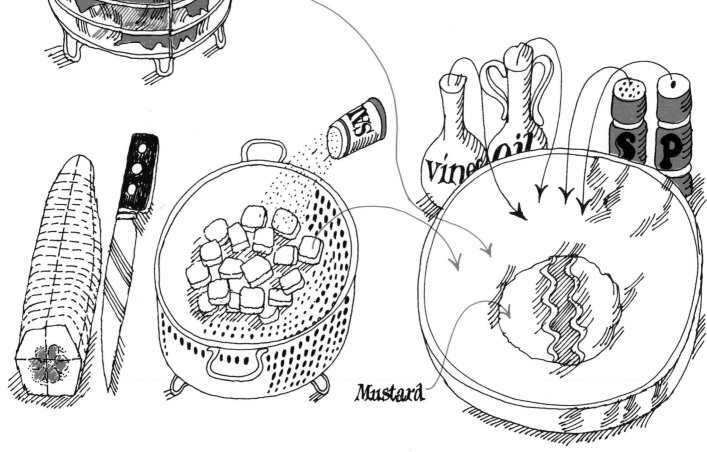

2 Peel the cucumber and cut into small cubes and
   place them in a colander. Sprinkle on some salt
   and leave to drain for at least 30 minutes. Rinse
   with cold water and leave to dry.

3 Mix the vinegar, oil, salt, pepper and dry
   mustard together in a salad bowl, add the
   spinach and the cucumber and toss together
   gently but thoroughly.

   Serve immediately.

100

SPINACH SALAD

A salad of good, earthy character, honest and
sincere. The combination of spinach and velvety
cucumber, plus the dressing, gives this salad a
distinctive taste all its own. It is zesty,
robust and highly nutritious.

It is the only way my children will eat spinach.
It provides an unusual accompaniment to any main course.

200–300 g (8–12 oz) lean, cooked, cold meat
   (leftover veal, beef, pork or lamb, cut into
   julienne strips about 25 mm (1 inch) long
   and 6 mm ($\frac{1}{4}$ inch) wide)
100 g (4 oz) green peas
1 large carrot, cooked and cubed
2 cold, boiled potatoes, cubed
2 gherkins, cubed
1 medium onion, cut into julienne strips
25 ml (1 fl oz) vinegar
3–4 tablespoons juice from gherkins
salt and pepper to taste
1 level teaspoon sugar
1 small carton sour cream
chopped parsley or chives for garnish

(Serves 4–6)

2 Make a marinade of vinegar, gherkin juice, salt and pepper and the sugar and pour it over the salad in the bowl.

1 Place all the meat and vegetables in a salad bowl.

3 Leave to marinate in the refrigerator for an hour or longer, tossing it once in a while.

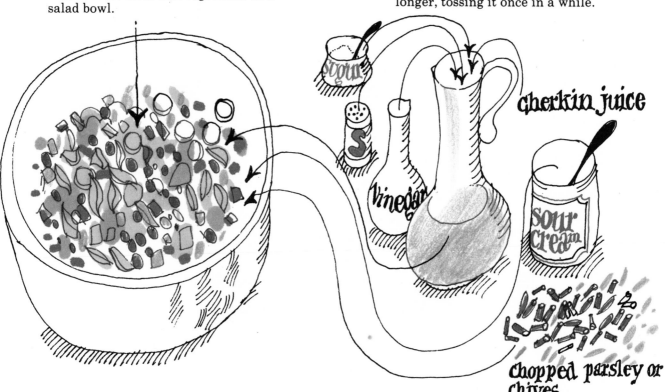

4 Then fold the sour cream in gently but thoroughly

5 Dust with chopped parsley or chives.

Note: This salad will keep for a day or two if tightly covered and kept in a refrigerator.

   You can also use cooked green beans, broad beans, capers, black or green olives, cooked beetroot or cooked mushrooms.

RUSSIAN SALAD

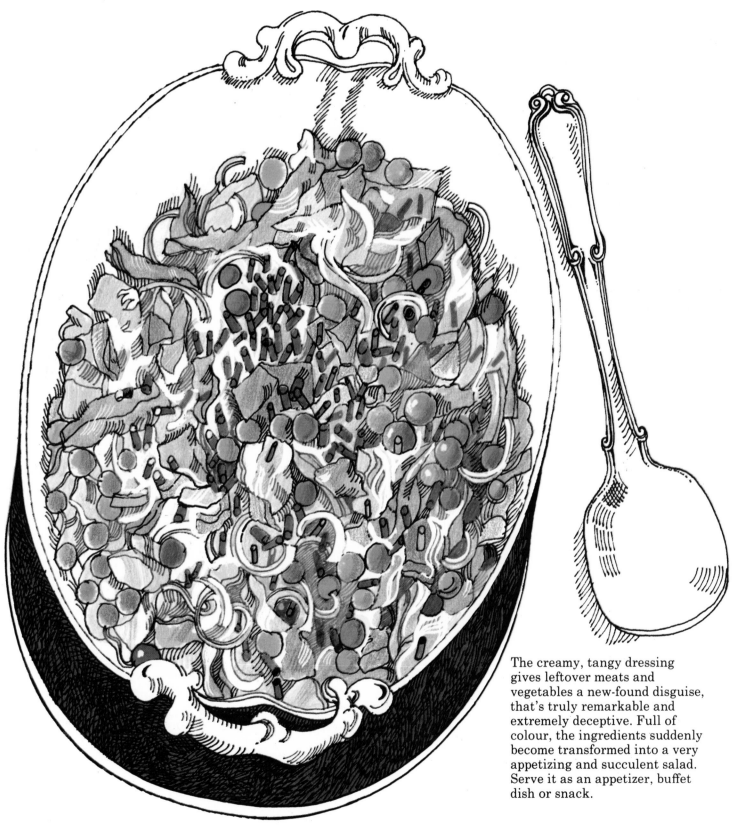

The creamy, tangy dressing
gives leftover meats and
vegetables a new-found disguise,
that's truly remarkable and
extremely deceptive. Full of
colour, the ingredients suddenly
become transformed into a very
appetizing and succulent salad.
Serve it as an appetizer, buffet
dish or snack.

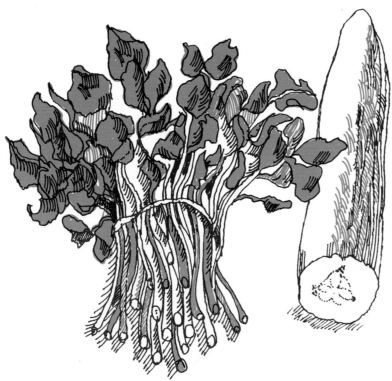

2 bunches watercress
½ cucumber, peeled and thinly sliced
100 g (4 oz) blue cheese, crumbled (optional)
3 tablespoons fresh lemon juice
8 tablespoons oil
salt and pepper to taste

(Serves 4)

1 Place the washed, trimmed and dried watercress in a salad bowl, add the sliced cucumber and the crumbled cheese (if used).

2 Toss it all together.

3 Into a screwtop jar put the lemon juice, oil, salt and pepper and shake it well until thoroughly mixed and thick and creamy.

crumbled cheese

P

S

cream

Dressing

oil

4 Pour this mixture over the salad, toss again gently.

Serve immediately!

Watercress Salad

This could be called a real English salad, in so far as watercress must be more readily available in England than anywhere else. The tangy lemon dressing gives this salad a smooth and delicate taste. Ideal as an accompaniment to any main course.

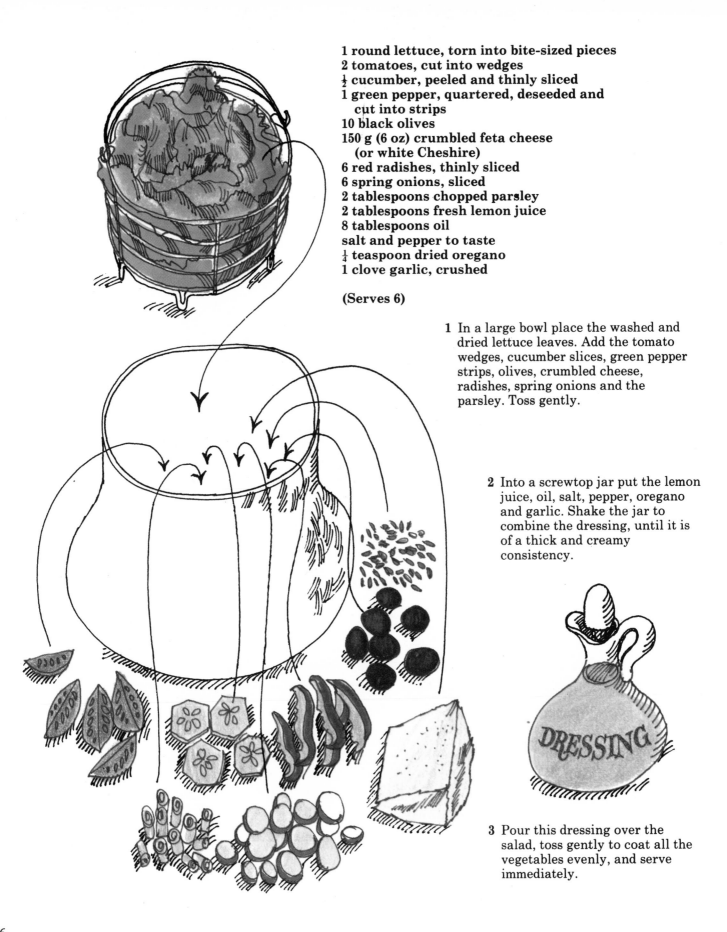

1 round lettuce, torn into bite-sized pieces
2 tomatoes, cut into wedges
½ cucumber, peeled and thinly sliced
1 green pepper, quartered, deseeded and
  cut into strips
10 black olives
150 g (6 oz) crumbled feta cheese
  (or white Cheshire)
6 red radishes, thinly sliced
6 spring onions, sliced
2 tablespoons chopped parsley
2 tablespoons fresh lemon juice
8 tablespoons oil
salt and pepper to taste
¼ teaspoon dried oregano
1 clove garlic, crushed

(Serves 6)

1 In a large bowl place the washed and
dried lettuce leaves. Add the tomato
wedges, cucumber slices, green pepper
strips, olives, crumbled cheese,
radishes, spring onions and the
parsley. Toss gently.

2 Into a screwtop jar put the lemon
juice, oil, salt, pepper, oregano
and garlic. Shake the jar to
combine the dressing, until it is
of a thick and creamy
consistency.

3 Pour this dressing over the
salad, toss gently to coat all the
vegetables evenly, and serve
immediately.

GREEK SALAD

As refreshing and stimulating as it looks, a perfect blend of vegetables and cheese. The lemon dressing gives it a good tangy taste, while the feta cheese provides an authentic Mediterranean flavour. However, if feta cheese is unavailable, do not despair, white Cheshire makes an adequate substitute.

Excellent as a first course or as a side dish. A favourite in our household.

107

200 g (8 oz) thick sliced bacon
oil for frying bacon
6 heads chicory
2 hard-boiled eggs, chopped
100 ml (4 fl oz) oil
25 ml (1 fl oz) vinegar
salt and pepper to taste
2 tablespoons chopped parsley

(Serves 4–6)

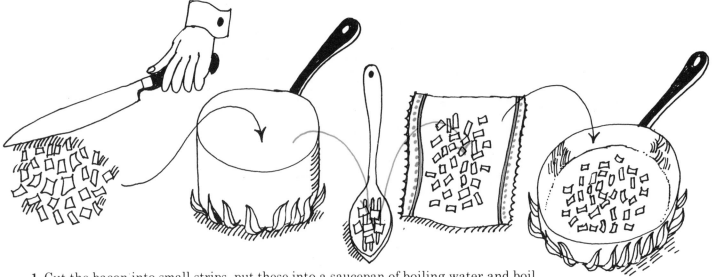

1 Cut the bacon into small strips, put these into a saucepan of boiling water and boil them for 10 minutes to reduce the saltiness. Remove them with a draining spoon and dry on a paper towel. When thoroughly dry, fry the strips in the oil in a frying pan until crisp.

chopped egg

2 Cut the chicory into 13 mm (½-inch) thick slices and place them in a salad bowl. Add the chopped egg.

3 Make up the dressing by mixing together the oil, vinegar, salt and pepper. Pour this mixture over the salad and toss it together gently but thoroughly.

4 Place it on a nice platter and sprinkle the bacon bits and parsley on top.

Serve very soon.

Flemish
Chicory Salad

A beautifully tangy flavour. Crisp and very
refreshing. An ideal combination of chicory, egg and bacon.
This salad goes well with any fried meats, chicken or fish.

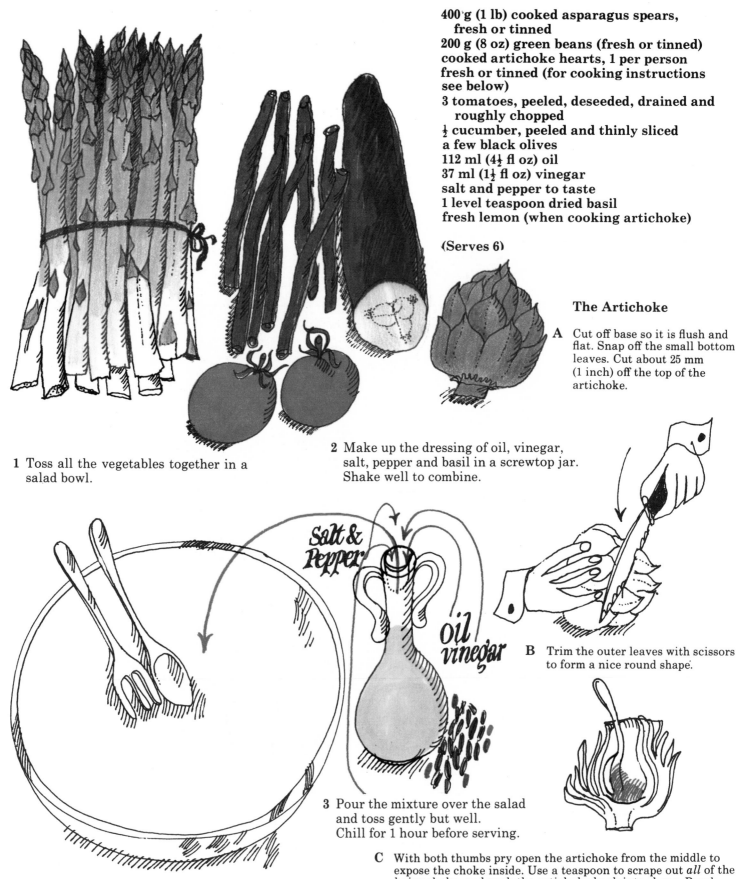

400 g (1 lb) cooked asparagus spears,
   fresh or tinned
200 g (8 oz) green beans (fresh or tinned)
cooked artichoke hearts, 1 per person
fresh or tinned (for cooking instructions
   see below)
3 tomatoes, peeled, deseeded, drained and
   roughly chopped
½ cucumber, peeled and thinly sliced
a few black olives
112 ml (4½ fl oz) oil
37 ml (1½ fl oz) vinegar
salt and pepper to taste
1 level teaspoon dried basil
fresh lemon (when cooking artichoke)

(Serves 6)

The Artichoke

A Cut off base so it is flush and
flat. Snap off the small bottom
leaves. Cut about 25 mm
(1 inch) off the top of the
artichoke.

1 Toss all the vegetables together in a
salad bowl.

2 Make up the dressing of oil, vinegar,
salt, pepper and basil in a screwtop jar.
Shake well to combine.

Salt & Pepper

oil vinegar

B Trim the outer leaves with scissors
to form a nice round shape.

3 Pour the mixture over the salad
and toss gently but well.
Chill for 1 hour before serving.

C With both thumbs pry open the artichoke from the middle to
expose the choke inside. Use a teaspoon to scrape out *all* of the
hairy choke, and push the artichoke back into shape. Brush
with lemon juice to prevent it discolouring and boil in salted
water for 15 minutes. Drain and leave to cool before using.

4 Toss again lightly, decorate with olives and serve
from the salad bowl or transfer it to a platter.

Italian Summer Salad

A real Italian salad – a typically Mediterranean combination. This is truly a magnificent recipe, grand enough to stand as an elegant starter, or it can make an unusual side dish to the main course.

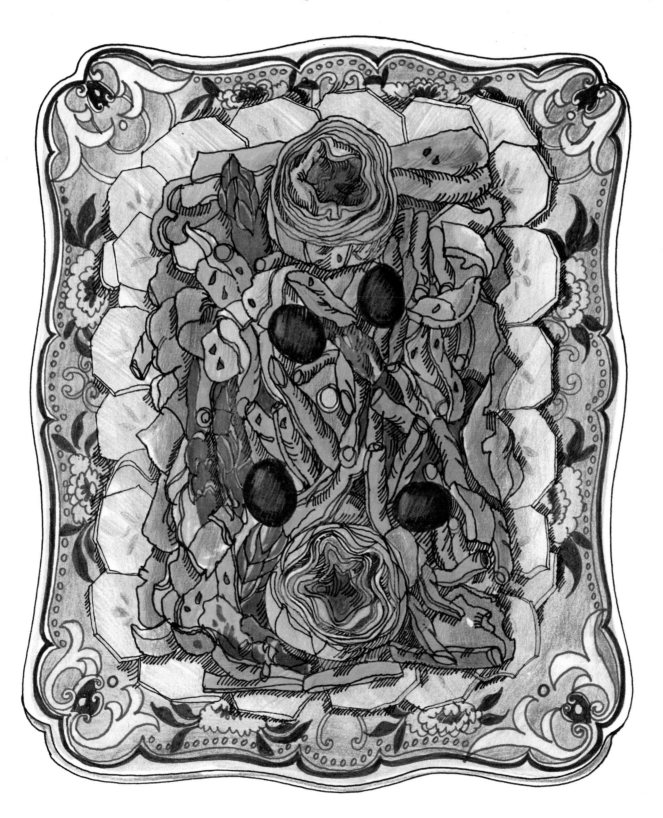

1 tin salmon
2 heaped tablespoons very finely
  chopped celery
2 hard-boiled eggs, chopped
4 tablespoons good mayonnaise
½ teaspoon curry powder

2 avocados
juice of 1 lemon
some nice lettuce leaves
paprika for garnish

(Serves 4)

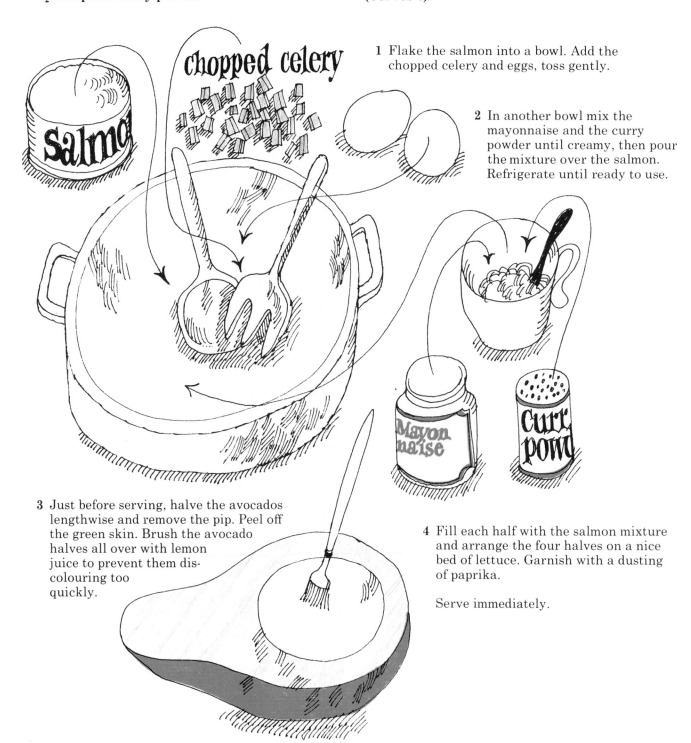

chopped celery

salmon

Mayonnaise

Curr powd

1 Flake the salmon into a bowl. Add the chopped celery and eggs, toss gently.

2 In another bowl mix the mayonnaise and the curry powder until creamy, then pour the mixture over the salmon. Refrigerate until ready to use.

3 Just before serving, halve the avocados lengthwise and remove the pip. Peel off the green skin. Brush the avocado halves all over with lemon juice to prevent them discolouring too quickly.

4 Fill each half with the salmon mixture and arrange the four halves on a nice bed of lettuce. Garnish with a dusting of paprika.

Serve immediately.

Salmon & Avocado Salad

This makes an excellent hors d'oeuvre winter and summer alike.
The smooth taste of the avocado blends ideally with the texture of
the salmon, eggs and celery. Very attractive to the eye, it can
grace any table with distinction.

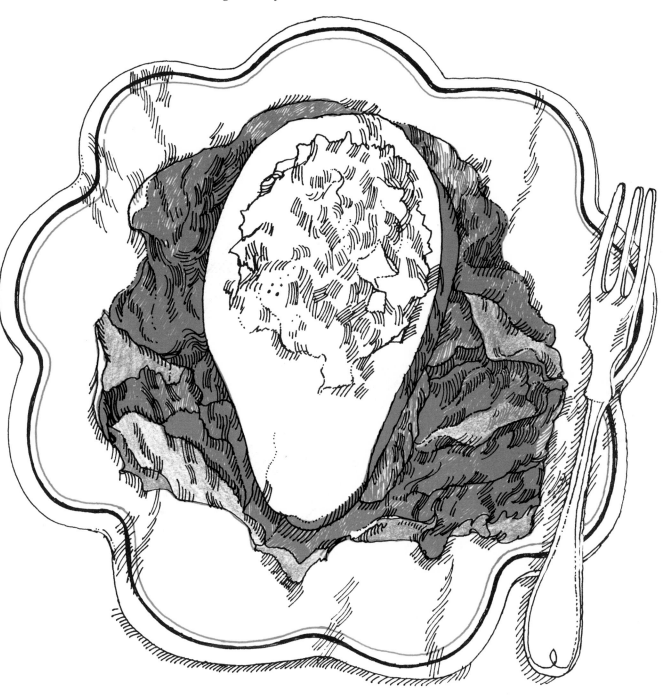

1 small cucumber
125 ml (5 fl oz) oil
62 ml (2½ fl oz) white wine vinegar
1 clove garlic, crushed
1 teaspoon dried basil
salt and pepper to taste
200 g (8 oz) button mushrooms
5 spring onions, chopped
2 tablespoons chopped parsley
1 green pepper, quartered, deseeded and
    cut into strips
3 tomatoes, cut into wedges

(Serves 4)

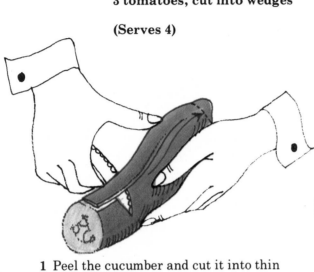

1 Peel the cucumber and cut it into thin slices.

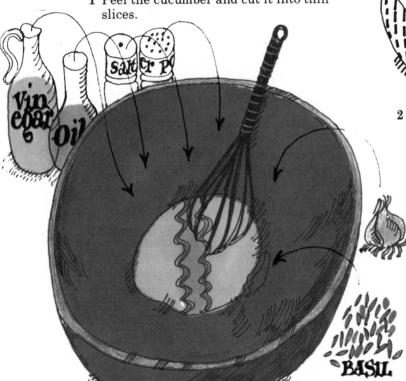

2 Place them in a colander, sprinkle some salt on top and leave to drain for 30 minutes. Rinse them with cold water and dry thoroughly.

3 In a large bowl make the dressing by combining the oil, vinegar, garlic, basil, salt and pepper thoroughly.

4 Add the whole mushrooms and chopped spring onions, the drained cucumber slices and parsley. Toss it all together gently. Chill in the refrigerator for an hour or more.

5 Place the tomato wedges over the salad in the bowl and over them the green pepper strips. Toss all the vegetables gently but thoroughly.

Serve immediately.

MEXICAN GAZPACHO SALAD

A super salad when served really fresh and slightly chilled. Juicy and refreshing. An ideal side dish to accompany any meat course. A very attractive salad to show off to your friends.

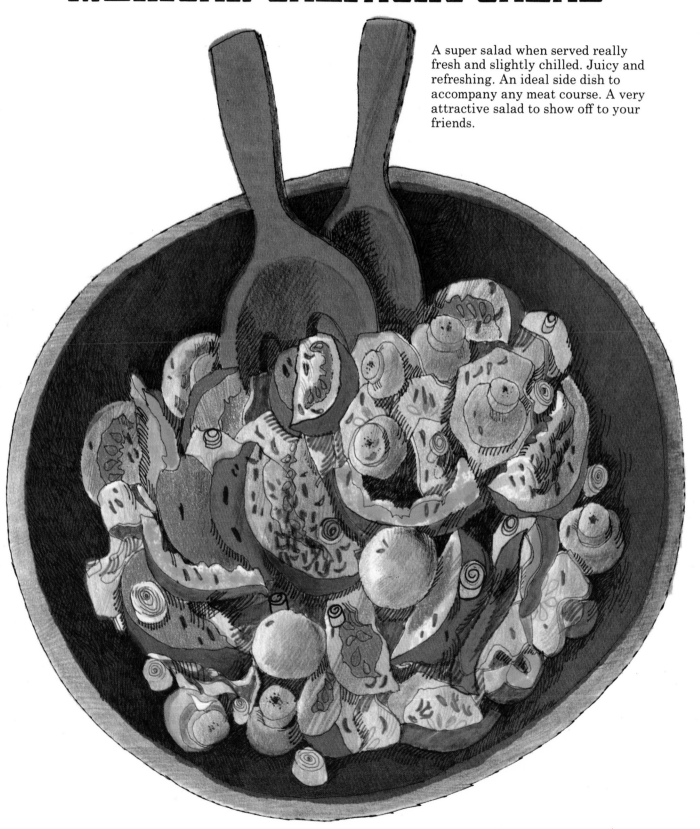

1 lettuce head
6 red radishes, cut into slices
2 tomatoes, cut into slices
2 celery stalks, chopped
½ cucumber, peeled and diced
6 stuffed green olives, sliced
1 bunch watercress, trimmed
200 g (8 oz) cooked shrimp
 (fresh or frozen)
8 tablespoons oil

4 tablespoons vinegar
salt and pepper to taste
1 teaspoon dried tarragon
1 green pepper, cut into rings and deseeded

(Serves 4–6)

1 Wash and dry the lettuce leaves and tear them into
 bite-sized pieces. Place them in a salad bowl.

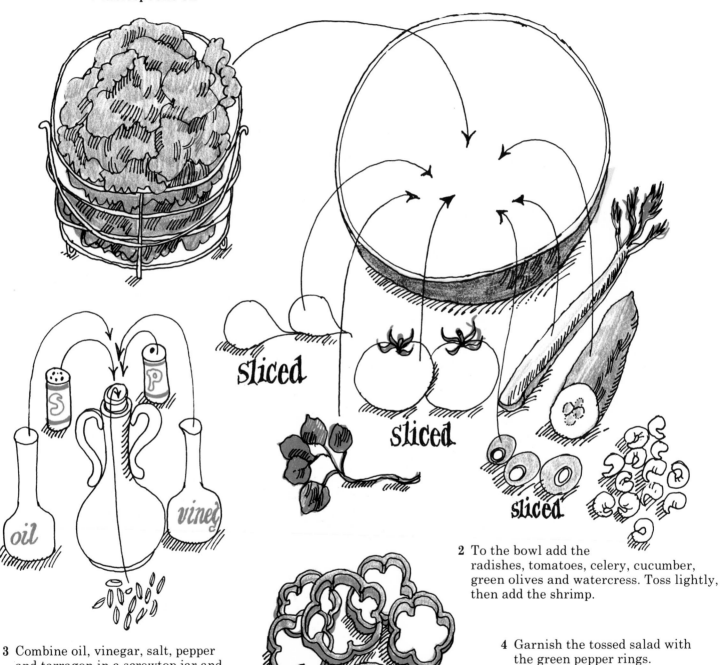

sliced

sliced

sliced

2 To the bowl add the
 radishes, tomatoes, celery, cucumber,
 green olives and watercress. Toss lightly,
 then add the shrimp.

3 Combine oil, vinegar, salt, pepper
 and tarragon in a screwtop jar and
 shake well to combine. Pour it over
 the salad and toss well.

4 Garnish the tossed salad with
 the green pepper rings.

 Serve immediately.

Shrimp Salad

An absolutely delicious salad, a beautiful starter to a summer dinner party. Serve it as a first course on small plates, with a garnish of crisp toast, or brown bread and butter.

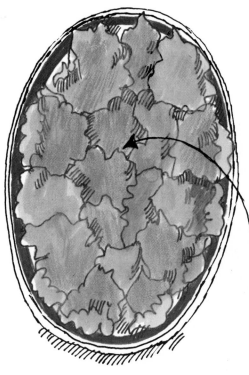

1 lettuce head
1 tin crabmeat or frozen crabmeat
 (as many servings as you will need)
6 heaped tablespoons good mayonnaise
4 tablespoons double cream
1 level desertspoon paprika
1 teaspoon Worcester sauce
5 spring onions, chopped
2 tablespoons fresh lemon juice
salt and pepper to taste
2 hard-boiled eggs, cut into wedges
lemon wedges
1 tablespoon chopped parsley

(Serves 2 for lunch and 4 as an hors d'oeuvre)

crabmeat

2 Place the crabmeat in the centre of the platter and pour over it this famous Louis dressing:

1 Arrange some nice large lettuce leaves on an attractive platter. Scatter the smaller leaves over them, or tear them into bite-sized pieces.

3 In a small bowl gently mix the mayonnaise, cream, paprika, Worcester sauce, spring onions, lemon juice, salt and pepper until well blended.

4 Garnish with wedges of hard-boiled egg and lemon and sprinkle with parsley.

Serve immediately.

118

CRAB SALAD LOUIS

A San Francisco classic, which has endeared itself to millions of Americans. The special dressing, together with the crab-meat, give a flavour typical of the San Francisco area. It can be served as a first course, or as a delightful summer lunch. Fresh and satisfying, its flavour more than justifies the relatively high cost.

SALAD DRESSINGS

Mayonnaise

1 egg yolk
¼ teaspoon dry mustard
salt and pepper to taste
pinch of sugar
2 tablespoons wine vinegar
125 ml (¼ pint) oil

Place the egg yolk, mustard, salt, pepper and sugar in a deep bowl. Mix until well combined. Add the vinegar and whisk it with a wooden spoon or wire whisk until white and frothy. Add the oil, slowly drop by drop, whisking constantly, until the oil is used.
Occasionally the mayonnaise will curdle. Start again in another bowl with just one egg yolk. Whisk it constantly and slowly and add the curdled mayonnaise to it, by the teaspoonful, until it is all smooth and creamy. If the mayonnaise seems too thick for your needs, thin it down with a little cream.
Mayonnaise can also be made in a mixer, just follow the directions in your mixer book. However, mayonnaise made in a mixer does not have the same shine and texture.

Green Goddess Dressing

1 quantity of mayonnaise as above
3 chopped anchovy fillets
3 spring onions, chopped
2 tablespoons chopped parsley
1 teaspoon dried tarragon
1 heaped tablespoon chopped chives
2 tablespoons wine vinegar

Mix all the ingredients until smooth and creamy. Refrigerate before using on any green salad.

Thousand Island Dressing

1 quantity of mayonnaise as above
62 ml (2½ fl oz) ketchup
8 stuffed olives, finely chopped
1 small green pepper, finely chopped
1 tablespoon finely chopped chives or onion
1 hard-boiled egg, chopped
1 tablespoon chopped parsley

Mix all the ingredients together until smooth and creamy. Refrigerate before using on any green salad.

Yogurt Dressing

1 carton yogurt
1 small clove garlic, crushed
½ teaspoon dried oregano
1 tablespoon oil
salt and pepper to taste
1 fresh lemon (juice only)

Mix well, until smooth, the yogurt, crushed garlic, oregano, oil, salt and pepper. Then stir in the lemon juice and blend until smooth and creamy (about 280 calories).

Creamy French Dressing

1 tablespoon paprika
1 teaspoon sugar
1 teaspoon salt
75 ml (3 fl oz) vinegar
1 raw egg
225 ml (9 fl oz) oil

Combine paprika, sugar and salt. Add the vinegar and the egg and beat well. Add the oil in a slow stream, beating all the time, until the mixture is thick and creamy. Chill before serving over any green salad.

Blue Cheese Dressing

1 clove garlic
100 g (4 oz) blue cheese
2 teaspoons Worcester sauce
juice of 1 lemon
½ teaspoon dry mustard
¼ teaspoon paprika
1 tablespoon oil
salt and pepper to taste
1 quantity of mayonnaise as above

Mash garlic and cheese in a bowl. Add the Worcester sauce, lemon juice, mustard, paprika, oil, salt and pepper. Blend well. Add the mayonnaise and stir until smooth and creamy. Refrigerate before using over any green salad.

Watercress Dressing

2 tablespoons fresh lemon juice
1 tablespoon wine vinegar
½ teaspoon dried tarragon
125 ml (5 fl oz) oil
salt and pepper to taste
1 bunch watercress

Mix lemon juice, vinegar, tarragon, oil, salt and pepper until well blended. Then stir in the bunch of watercress, finely chopped. Use over any green salad.

Low Calorie Dressing

200 g (8 oz) cottage cheese
125 ml (5 fl oz) milk
salt and pepper to taste
2 tablespoons fresh lemon juice
1 small green pepper, chopped
5 spring onions, chopped
1 clove garlic, crushed

You can best do this in a mixer. Just swirl all the ingredients around until well blended. Refrigerate before using on any green salad.
If a mixer is not available, force the cottage cheese through a fine sieve and add all the other ingredients to it. Blend until smooth (about 350 calories).

PASTA CONTENTS

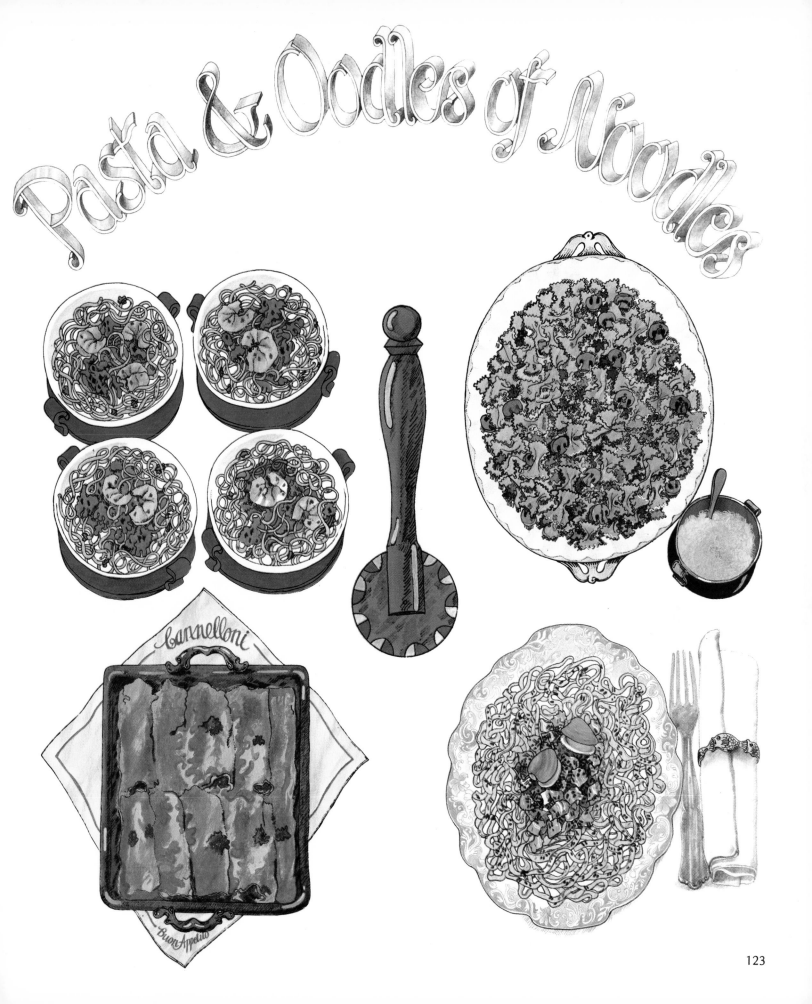

Pasta & Oodles of Noodles

Cannelloni

Buon Appetito

Introduction

Pasta – from where did it come?

The legend that pasta was introduced into Italy by Marco Polo seems to be largely a myth, for there is no real historical evidence to support it. It is much more likely that pasta was eaten by the Romans long before Marco Polo's travels to China.

However, the evolution of pasta has been typically Italian. Where else could such a basic staple as pasta have found expression in so many different forms and variations? Many, with their beautifully sculptured shapes, are like miniature works of art. All touched by the Italian genius for synthesising art and life. For Italians pasta is not so much a meal as a way of life – such is their passion for pasta, with its many colourful and regional variations.

It is sad that pasta cooking has been unappreciated in this country for so long. Unfortunately many people believe that pasta amounts to nothing more than spaghetti, macaroni, ravioli and something served in the local Italian restaurant called lasagne. Alas, what masquerades as a pasta dish in many so-called Italian restaurants is at the very best a pale imitation of the real thing. Genuine pasta cooking provides food which is immensely versatile, enormously satisfying, tasty, inexpensive, nutritious, easy to prepare and, contrary to popular belief, low in calories – at least in the sense that a little pasta goes a long way, leaving the stomach full and contented for hours.

The joys of pasta can be as complex or as simple as you like – many Italians treasure a dish of spaghetti tossed in olive oil with a grating of black pepper. If you want to prepare really authentic pasta, try making your own dough. Homemade pasta may sound like a near impossibility – but it is not. It can be mastered very quickly for it requires no special skills, just patience and a little practice. Once mastered the results are most gratifying. Exquisite homemade ravioli with a filling of juicy, delicately flavoured meat, or aromatic cheeses, or cannelloni, stuffed with a succulent beef and spinach filling; or tortellini with a characteristic Italian filling of ricotta cheese.

There are also the delights of regional sauces, with their pungent flavour of fresh basil, (it is worth giving up a little corner of your garden to grow it) and the ever famous and versatile Bolognese sauce.

Throughout this book you will find a collection of traditional recipes which echo the flavour and sumptuous delights of Italian cooking. In selecting the recipes an attempt has been made to balance the many regional flavours of Italian cooking, using only the traditional ingredients – although you may find it necessary to compromise from time to time. Taking into account the availability of certain ingredients I have indicated alternatives when it might seem necessary.

We hope this book reflects our love of pasta, for selecting the recipes and preparing the drawings has been an absolute delight, to which our stomachs can well testify. Our Look and Cook format has been devised for ease of use and understanding, so that the reader can comprehend at a glance how a dish is prepared, and how it should look when finally it reaches the dinner table.

As a footnote to this introduction we would like to express our grateful thanks and appreciation to our publishers for their kindness in allowing us to produce this book. We are also indebted to many friends who have offered suggestions in the preparation of the manuscript. In particular our old friends Carla and Frankie Mondolfo in Rome, and Elizabeth Cox in London – their assistance has been invaluable.

Lastly, we hope the reader will find this book a practical, no-nonsense kind of cookbook. One to be looked at and enjoyed, but above all, to be used.

Buon Appetito!

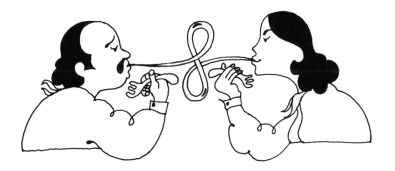

How to Please Your Pasta

(and make oodles of beautiful noodles)

A basic guide to some of the Do's and Don'ts of pasta cooking.

Pasta Making

Bought pasta, even the ones produced over here, are usually of excellent quality. However, like most other commercially produced foods, it is never quite as good as the homemade kind. So I feel everyone should give pasta-making a try. It is not as difficult as it may sound, and is a very satisfying occupation. Of course pasta-making is a necessary task for the preparation of ravioli and tortellini. These are of doubtful quality when bought.

Making the dough is really easy. Rolling it out requires a little practice. If you are doing it for the first time, don't make it on a busy day. Slowly does it. And remember to keep your working surface well floured at all times. Pasta dough gets quite sticky when it is rolled out. There is no need to worry about too much flour sticking to the dough – it will all come off in the cooking water.

To make egg-noodle dough

4 large eggs

4 tablespoons cold water

about 400 gm (1 lb) plain flour

1 Break the eggs into a large mixing bowl. Add the water and about a quarter of the flour. Beat this mixture with a wire whisk until it is very smooth.

2 Add nearly all the rest of the flour and work the mixture with your hands into a soft dough. If the dough seems sticky, work in the rest of the flour. (The absorbency of the flour can vary from one bag to the next, as can the size of the eggs.)

3 Turn the dough out onto a kneading surface and knead it well for 10 minutes, just as you would a bread dough. This will extract the gluten contents in the flour and give the dough its elasticity.

4 Put the dough back in the bowl, cover it and leave it to rest for at least 20 minutes. (There is no way in which the dough can be rolled out until *after* a lengthy rest period; it will just pull back on you.)

5 Roll the dough out to a thickness of 3 mm ($\frac{1}{8}$ inch). You may find it easier to cut the dough into two pieces first, and roll them out separately. They will be more manageable that way.

To make green-noodle dough

1 250 gm (10 oz) packet frozen spinach, cooked and chopped or 400 gm (1 lb) fresh spinach, cooked and chopped

4 large eggs

300–400 gm (12–16 oz) plain flour

1 Drain the cooked spinach well and squeeze as much as possible to remove the cooking water. The more expert you are at this, the less flour you will need and your noodles will be greener.

2 Break the eggs into a mixing bowl. Add the spinach and a quarter of the flour. Beat well with a wire whisk until the mixture is smooth.

3 Add the rest of the flour gradually, then follow the instructions for egg-noodle dough from stage 2.

Pasta by Machine

For those cooks who become pasta addicts, it is well worth acquiring a pasta machine. The machines make an excellent job of kneading and rolling out the pasta and cutting the noodles. It need not be an expensive machine either. The cheaper ones are just as efficient at rolling out the dough, but they have fewer blades and do not cut quite as many different shapes. But they all cut egg noodles and flat sheets – really the basic requirements.

Shaping of Pasta

Shaping the pasta is the fun part. There are hundreds of different pasta shapes. The basic ones are passed through dies and emerge as solid, long rods. These are spaghetti of various thicknesses. The next step is to push a metal rod through the solid strand, and these emerge as macaroni. Then come all the fancy shapes of twists, curls, shells, rings, ribbons, tubes, stars, etc. The easiest and most popular ones to make at home are those cut from flat sheets of pasta, and are then called noodles. You make these as follows:

Roll the flat sheet of dough up from one side to the other, like a swiss roll, and cut slices off it with a sharp knife. Unroll the slices and lay the noodles flat on a piece of well floured waxed, or greaseproof, paper. Leave them to dry for 10–15 minutes before cooking.

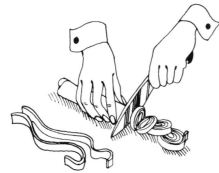

For tagliatelle: cut the roll into 12 mm (½ inch) slices
For fettuccine: cut the roll into 6 mm (¼ inch) slices
For fettucce: cut the roll into 12–18 mm (½–¾ inch) slices

Pappardelle are cut from a flat sheet of dough into strips of about 16 mm (⅝ inch) widths. Cut them with a fluted pastry wheel rather than a knife, this will give the noodles their characteristic edges. Dry them for only 5 minutes before cooking.

Also from flat sheets are cut the following:
manicotti: cut into 76 mm (3 inch) squares
lasagne: cut into 100 × 255 (4 × 10 inch) rectangles
cannelloni: cut into 100 mm (4 inch) squares (Don't dry any of these; cook them as soon as you can.)

Any leftover pasta dough can be gathered into a ball and rolled out again, to be cut into noodles, or it can be cut into small squares for soups. These are called pastina or quadrucci.

Storing Pasta

Noodles which are not cooked straight away after the specified drying period should be left out on floured, waxed paper until they are completely dry. This takes at least one day. They will then resemble commercially produced pasta and should be stored as such, in paper bags or cardboard boxes, to allow for air circulation. Dried pasta will keep for months without refrigeration.

Filled pasta such as ravioli and tortellini cannot be dried because the filling will spoil. They can however be frozen. Wrap them tightly so that they will not touch, or they will stick together. Flour them well before wrapping.

Cooking of Pasta

Pasta needs to be cooked in a large pot, with plenty of water to float around in. It should never be crowded into a pot or it will stick together. For the same reason you should not use a metal spoon for stirring; a wooden spoon, or better still, a wooden fork does a much more efficient job.

As a rule 400 gm (1 lb) of pasta requires at least 500 ml (8 pints) of water and 1 tablespoon of salt. But do not add the salt until the water boils, and only just before the pasta goes in, otherwise you get an odd side-taste. The pot should never be more than partially covered.

Long, thin pasta should not be broken into pieces. Immerse it as far as it will go in boiling water, let it fan out at the top. Then bend in the middle and force the rest under water with a wooden fork. Other pastas should all go into the pot at the same time, otherwise some of it will be cooked more quickly than the rest, and nothing is as bad as pasta which has been boiled too long.

Bought pasta cooks much longer than fresh, homemade pasta. Follow the packet directions, or better still, bite a piece now and then. The pasta should be soft, but with a slight resilience in the centre. This is the *al dente* stage, and the stage at which most Italians serve their pasta. However, you may like yours a little bit harder or softer than that. But bear in mind, it should never be mushy.

Homemade, fresh pasta cooks very fast:

Egg noodles, yellow	5–6 minutes approximately
Egg noodles, green	4–5 minutes approximately
Lasagne noodles	2 minutes
Manicotti	2 minutes
Cannelloni	2 minutes
Tortellini	5–8 minutes
Ravioli	5–8 minutes

These are rough guides, the best guides are your teeth. As a general rule, homemade pasta is cooked when it rises to the top of the pot.

Pasta Serving

Most commonly pasta used to be served as a first or second course, to be followed by the main course or entrée. It is still frequently served this way in many restaurants in Italy, but at home it has become more of a main dish.

If pasta is served as a first course, 50–75 gm (2–3 oz) of pasta per person is plenty. It should then be served in rimmed, small bowls and eaten with just a fork.

However, if pasta is served as a main course, you have to judge the amount of pasta per person by their appetites. Main-meal pasta can be served on a dinner plate, and it makes a delicious satisfying and usually inexpensive meal when served with some fresh, crusty bread and a crisp, tossed salad. Followed by some fresh fruit, it is one of the most nutritious meals you can serve.

Cheeses for Pasta

The most commonly used cheeses in pasta cookery are cheeses which are used grated. The two most popular and easily obtainable of these are Parmesan and Romano, in that order. Ideally it is best to use the imported ones, for their quality is immensely superior to the domestic variety. However, if you cannot get the imported kinds, domestic brands are adequate. Real imported Parmesan should be at least three years old and golden in colour. Romano cheese is white.

Neither cheese should ever be bought already grated. Once grated they soon lose their pungency and taste like plastic – no complement to a lovingly prepared dish. Do not grate the cheeses until just before you plan to use them.

Grated Parmesan is passed with just about every dish of pasta, except fishy ones, where its sharp flavour would distract too much from the delicate taste of the fish.

Ricotta cheese is used mainly as a filling in stuffed pasta and is readily available in most large supermarkets. Cottage cheese – which looks similar – is only a substitute, and should only be used if ricotta is absolutely unavailable.

Mozzarella cheese is commonly used in baked dishes, since it acquires its characteristic stringiness only when it is hot. It is a mild, somewhat creamy, cheese.

Ingredients in Pasta Cooking

Most of the different kinds of pasta used in this book are easily obtainable. If however you have trouble tracking down a particular shape of pasta, persistent chasing of your grocer should bring results. If he is not willing to satisfy you, write to Pasta Foods, St. Albans, Herts. They are one of the major suppliers of pasta and will be sure to help.

The herbs in this book are also readily available in dried form. Fresh ones are never seen in supermarkets, but they are great fun to grow in the garden or in a flowerpot.

Most people believe that the Italians use a lot more garlic than they do. Indeed many use it only sparingly. Then there are people who consider garlic in a sautéed form too heavy to digest, and prefer to add it later, together with the tomatoes. See which method you prefer. There is also a rule that if a dish contains tomatoes, any cooking oil can be used for the sauté stage. However, if a dish does not contain tomatoes, olive oil is essential for enhancing the authentic flavours.

Any pasta used in this book can be exchanged for another shape of pasta if desired. There are no hard and fast rules as to what goes with what. Personally I do prefer the larger pasta shapes with those succulent meat sauces, so the sauce will cling to the grooves, little bits of meat get stuck in the crevices and fill up the inside – delicious!

The meat contents in my recipes are usually rather higher than Italian cookbooks suggest. This is because I believe that most people will want to serve pasta as a main course – as indeed a lot of Italians do. So the nutritional value of the dishes has been taken into account. One hundred grams (4 oz) of meat per person does not seem extravagant. Italian cookbooks usually suggest 50 gm (2 oz) per person. I prefer to give up 'authenticity' for 'nutritional value' here.

Of course the pasta itself, even the bought variety, has a high nutritional value, being made of good flour or semolina flour with wholesome additions of spinach or eggs, or both.

Note I like to pour off the accumulated fat by setting the lid askew, only leaving a tiny crack for the fat to escape through. You can pour the hot fat straight down the sink, provided the cold tap is running. The cold water will flush the globules down smoothly.

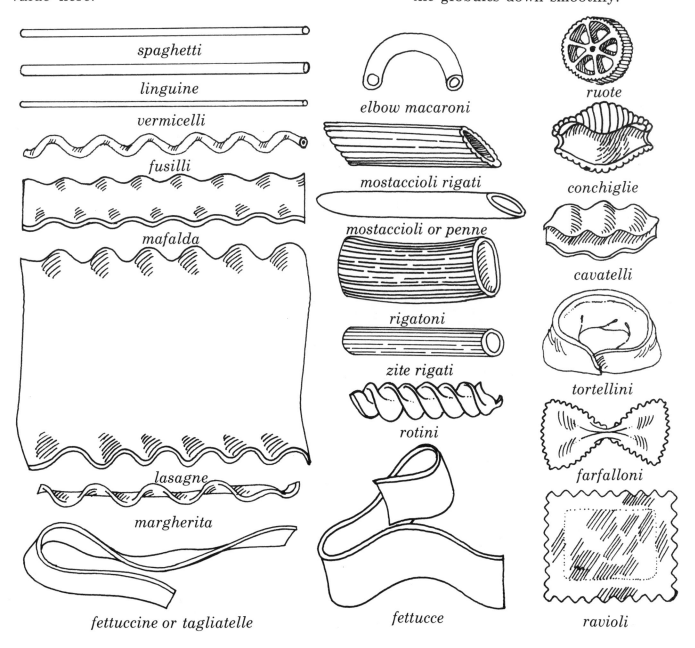

spaghetti

linguine

vermicelli

fusilli

mafalda

lasagne

margherita

fettuccine or tagliatelle

elbow macaroni

mostaccioli rigati

mostaccioli or penne

rigatoni

zite rigati

rotini

fettucce

ruote

conchiglie

cavatelli

tortellini

farfalloni

ravioli

37 gm (1½ oz) butter
4 rashers unsmoked bacon
1 large onion, finely chopped
1 medium carrot, finely chopped
1 stalk celery, finely chopped
2 tablespoons oil
130 gm (⅓ lb) minced beef
130 gm (⅓ lb) minced pork
130 gm (⅓ lb) minced veal

100 ml (4 fl oz) white wine
½ litre (1 pint) good beef stock
3 tablespoons tomato purée
1 teaspoon dried oregano
little grated nutmeg
salt and pepper to taste
250 ml (½ pint) double cream (or to taste)
400 gm (1 lb) spaghetti
grated Parmesan cheese

1   Melt the butter in a frying pan and in it sauté the chopped bacon, onion, carrot and celery. Cook, uncovered, stirring frequently, for about 10 minutes.
Set aside till needed.

finely chopped   bacon chopped   finely chopped   finely chopped

2   Heat the oil in a heavy saucepan and in it brown the meats, breaking up any lumps with a wooden spoon, until the mixture is brown and crumbly. Pour off the accumulated fat using the saucepan lid.

nutmeg   beef   veal   pork

3   Put back on the fire and stir in the wine. Cook it over high heat until most of the wine has evaporated. Stir in the beef stock, tomato purée, oregano, nutmeg, salt and pepper, and the reserved vegetables and bacon.

4   Simmer this sauce, only partially covered, until it has reduced to a thick sauce, about 40–60 minutes. Add all or some of the cream, but do not boil again!

5   Cook the spaghetti in plenty of boiling water (add salt when boiling) until *al dente*. Drain.

SPAGHETTI

6   Serve the pasta on hot plates, with some of the sauce spooned on top. Serve plenty of grated Parmesan cheese with this dish.

Note   This sauce is equally good over any noodle or macaroni, or any of the larger pasta shapes, such as rigatoni or shells.

Spaghetti Bolognese

As a child this was probably your first introduction to pasta – or so you thought. A familiar name, but have you tried the authentic version? The smooth and delicate tasting bolognese sauce is distinguished by the addition of fresh cream and aromatic vegetables. Savour this simple dish and discover the real thing, Bologna Style. The children will love it! (Serves 4)

50 gm (2 oz) butter
125 ml (¼ pint) double cream
6 tablespoons grated Parmesan cheese
salt and pepper to taste
200 gm (8 oz) fettucce

1 Melt the butter in a small saucepan over a low flame. Don't let it brown.

3 Cook the fettucce in plenty of boiling water (add salt when boiling) until *al dente*. Drain well.

FETTUCCE

DRAIN

PARMESAN

S P

2 Off the heat add the cream and the grated Parmesan. Put back on the cooker to heat the sauce through and melt the cheese. Do not boil, however, because of the fresh cream. Stir in the salt and pepper.

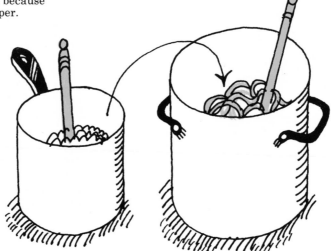

4 Combine the noodles and the sauce and leave to stand, covered, for 2 minutes before serving.

Pass more grated Parmesan cheese if you wish.

Note   You can substitute fettuccine for fettucce. Homemade noodles are especially fine for this dish.

FETTUCCE ALFREDO

This dish is named after Alfredo, owner of the famous
restaurant *Alfredo* in Rome. It makes an extremely delicious
hors d'oeuvre for four, and it is so easy to prepare.
One of the pure pasta dishes that distinguish themselves by the earthy
simplicity, it has a delicate, unbelievably creamy taste
and makes a great accompaniment to fried, grilled or roast meats.

1 recipe egg-noodle dough
1 small onion, finely chopped
2 tablespoons oil
1–2 cloves garlic, crushed
400 gm (1 lb) minced beef
2 tablespoons grated Parmesan cheese
2 tablespoons chopped parsley
1 teaspoon salt
little grated nutmeg
1 packet frozen spinach, cooked and chopped
    or 400 gm (1 lb) fresh spinach, cooked and chopped
2 eggs
1 recipe Salsa di Pomodori

1   To prepare the filling, sauté the onion in the oil
    until soft and transparent. Add the garlic and sauté
    1 minute longer. Add the minced beef, turn up
    the heat slightly, and brown the beef nicely.
    Break up any lumps with a wooden spoon. When
    cooked, transfer the mixture to a mixing bowl.

2   To the meat
    mixture add the cheese, pars-
    ley, salt, nutmeg, spinach and the eggs.
    Mix with a fork until well combined.

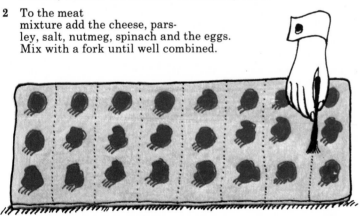

3   Divide the dough into 2 pieces, and roll each one out
    to a rectangle of 2 mm (⅛ inch) thickness.

4   Place a heaped teaspoon of filling at 50-mm (2-inch) intervals
    on one of the sheets of dough. With a pastry brush dipped in
    cold water, dampen a line on the space between the fillings to
    help seal the ravioli later. Cover the fillings with the other
    sheet of dough.

5   With your index finger press
    down between the fillings to
    seal them in. With the help of
    a fluted pastry wheel or a sharp

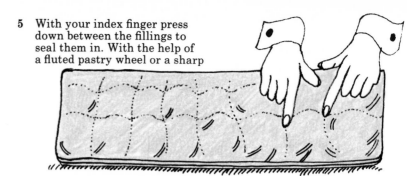

knife, cut the ravioli into 50-mm (2-inch) squares.
Seal the edges firmly by pressing the
seams together all around, either with
your finger or with a fork. Set the
ravioli aside on a well floured wax
paper until all ravioli have been made.

6   Cook the ravioli, a few at a time, in plenty of boil-
    ing water (add salt when boiling) until *al dente*
    (8–10 minutes). Drain them by removing them with a
    slotted spoon and proceed to boil the rest
    of the ravioli.

7   Spread a thin layer of tomato
    sauce in a baking dish or a deep, ovenproof platter. Lay the
    cooked ravioli loosely in the dish, in a single layer.
    This keeps the ravioli from sticking together. Cover each layer
    with more tomato sauce. Pour any leftover sauce over the whole dish.

8   To heat the ravioli through, bake the dish, covered with foil, in an oven
    preheated to 325°F, gas 3 (170°C). (Remember, they are already cooked.)
    This will take between 20 and 40 minutes, depending on how cold they
    were when put into the oven.

Note   Up to stage 7, ravioli can be made 2–3 hours in advance.

A magnificent combination of robust tomato sauce and beef filling gives this dish a full-bodied country flavour. Home-made, old-fashioned goodness. Make them yourself and find out what real home-made Italian ravioli are like. You will surprise and delight family and friends. (Serves 4)

135

This is the quantity per person:
1 tablespoon olive oil
3 rashers lean bacon (preferably unsmoked)
cut into strips
1 beaten egg
1 heaped teaspoon chopped parsley (optional)
a generous grating of black pepper
75 gm (3 oz) penne
2 tablespoons grated Romano or Parmesan cheese

1 Heat the oil in a saucepan and in it fry the bacon pieces until nicely browned. Remove the bacon with a draining spoon and leave to drain on paper towels.

4 Boil the penne in plenty of salted water until *al dente*. Do *not* drain! With a draining spoon remove the pasta from the water, letting it drain as much as you can. Then drop the steaming hot pasta into the egg mixture. The idea is to keep the pasta so hot that it will set the egg slightly. Mix it all up well.

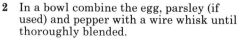

5 Sprinkle on the bacon bits and the Romano cheese and toss well.
Serve immediately, with more grated Romano if liked.

2 In a bowl combine the egg, parsley (if used) and pepper with a wire whisk until thoroughly blended.

3 Keep the egg mixture in a warm place until ready to use. (Not too hot though, or the egg would set.)

This dish is one of the most popular in Italy. And it is fast gaining popularity all over the world. It is one of the quickest and cheapest of pasta dishes. So full of goodness that it can be enjoyed as a main course. Truly delightful.

PENNE ALLA CARBONARA

½ recipe egg-noodle dough, cut
   into lasagne
   or **200 gm (½ lb) bought lasagne noodles**
1 recipe Ragù Bolognese
1 recipe Besciamella
5 tablespoons grated Parmesan cheese

1 Cook the lasagne, a few at a time, in plenty of boiling water
(add *salt* when boiling) until *al dente*. Drain them
in a colander and leave to cool slightly.

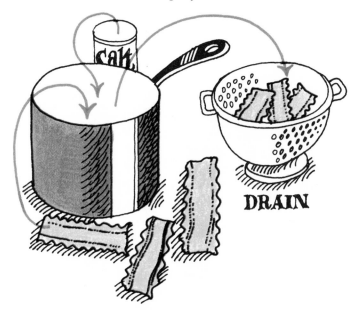

DRAIN

2 Butter generously a large baking dish or casserole
about $525 \times 690 \times 175$ mm ($9 \times 12 \times 3$ inches).

Bolognese Sauce

Besciamella

3 Spread a thin layer of Ragù Bolognese over the bottom
of the baking dish. Over it spread ⅓ of the Besciamella.
On top of that layer ⅓ of the cooked noodles, slightly
overlapping. Repeat this process, until all the sauces
have been used. Finish with a layer of Besciamella.
Onto the finished dish sprinkle the Parmesan cheese.
(Depending on the size of your dish, there may be
a few noodles left over.)

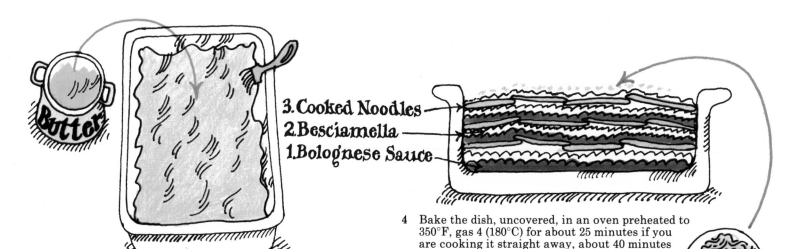

Butter

3. Cooked Noodles
2. Besciamella
1. Bolognese Sauce

4 Bake the dish, uncovered, in an oven preheated to
350°F, gas 4 (180°C) for about 25 minutes if you
are cooking it straight away, about 40 minutes
if it has been allowed to go cold.

Note   You can prepare stages 1–3 up to 3 hours in advance.
Cover the dish with foil or plastic wrap, until ready to bake.

Parmesan

Lasagne

One of the most substantial of all pasta dishes. Extremely popular both in Italy and abroad. A delectable blend of pasta, Besciamella and Ragù Bolognese makes this dish rich and appetizing. Full of nourishment, it takes a little time to prepare, but is more than worth the trouble. A delightful winter meal, which you will want to come back to even in summer. (Serves 4)

2–4 cloves garlic, cut in half
½ teaspoon dried red pepper flakes
2 tablespoons chopped parsley
5 tablespoons olive oil
400 gm (1 lb) thin spaghetti
freshly ground black pepper to taste

2   Cook the spaghetti in plenty of boiling water
(add salt when boiling) until *al dente*. Drain.

1   Sauté the garlic, red pepper flakes and the parsley
in the olive oil for 1–2 minutes over a low heat.
Do not let the garlic brown!
Remove the garlic with a slotted spoon and discard.

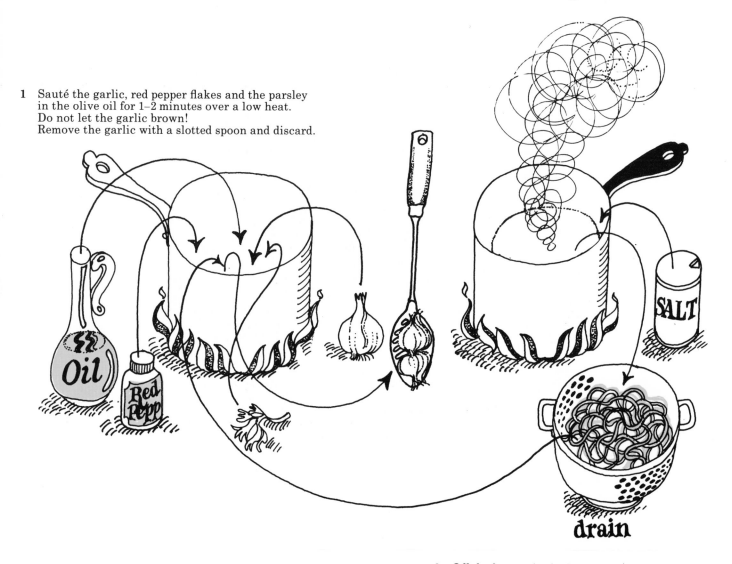

drain

3   Off the heat, mix the hot pasta into the hot oil mixture,
season with black pepper and mix well.

Serve immediately, absolutely piping hot!

Spaghetti Aglio e Olio

One of the pure and basic pasta dishes of Italy. A simple, ingenious combination of garlic and olive oil gives this dish its smooth quality. Extremely quick to make, tasty and inexpensive.

An authentic touch of Italy. Try it with a glass of chianti and some hearty conversation. Absolutely delicious!
(Serves 6 as an hors d'oeuvre) 141

1 medium onion, finely chopped
50 gm (2 oz) butter
200 gm (8 oz) mushrooms,
    sliced and the stems chopped
salt and pepper to taste
200 gm (8 oz) unsmoked ham *or* prosciutto,
    cut into squares
250 ml (½ pint) double cream (or to taste)
2 tablespoons chopped parsley
150 gm (6 oz) green noodles
150 gm (6 oz) yellow noodles
6 tablespoons grated Parmesan cheese

1 Sauté the onion in the butter
    until soft and transparent.

5 Cook the green and yellow noodles separately in plenty of
    boiling water (add salt when boiling) until *al dente*.
    Drain well. (Green noodles cool faster than yellow.)

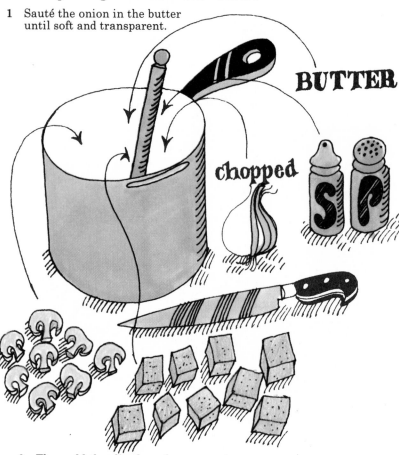

BUTTER

chopped

2 Then add the sliced mushrooms and
    chopped stems, turn up the heat
    slightly and sauté them until done, about 5 minutes.
    Stir frequently.

3 Add the salt and pepper and the ham squares and cook it
    all together another minute, just to heat through.

4 Add the cream and let everything heat through again, without
    letting the sauce boil. (Be especially careful if using fresh cream,
    it will tend to curdle.)
    Then stir in the parsley.

cream

EGG NOODLES
GREEN NOODLES
salt

parmesan

6 Combine the sauce with the noodles, add the Parmesan and
    stir well. Leave them, covered, for 2 minutes before serving.
    You can serve more grated Parmesan cheese at the table
    if you wish.

Note You can use all yellow noodles for this dish.

Paglia e Fieno

A beautifully creamy dish, full of different tastes,
textures and colours. An extremely ingenious blend that is as appealing to the eye
as it is to the tongue. Makes a great main course that's easy to make and never fails to please. (Serves 4)

62 gm (2½ oz) butter
2 tablespoons flour
200 ml (8 fl oz) milk
75 gm (3 oz) Gouda cheese
75 gm (3 oz) Gruyère cheese
75 gm (3 oz) mozzarella cheese
300 gm (12 oz) mostaccioli
50 gm (2 oz) butter
generous grating of black pepper
75 gm (3 oz) grated Parmesan cheese

3 Cook the mostaccioli in plenty of boiling water (add salt when boiling) until *al dente*. Drain. Transfer them to a hot dish, flake the remaining butter into them and toss the pasta well.

4 Re-heat the cheese sauce if it has cooled too much, and stir to make sure all the cheeses have melted.

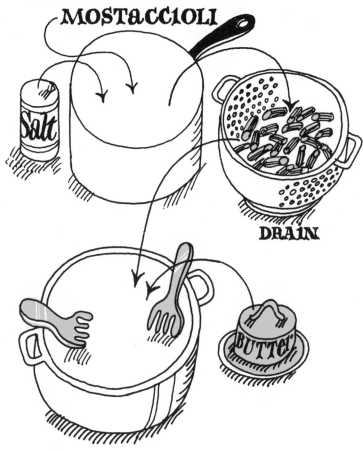

1 To make a white sauce, melt the 62 gm butter in a saucepan, add the flour all at once, and stir it around until all the flour has been absorbed into the butter. Then add the milk slowly, stirring all the time with a wire whisk, until the sauce starts to thicken. Simmer gently, stirring all the time, for 2 minutes.

5 Pour this sauce over the pasta, sprinkle on the pepper and toss well to distribute the sauce evenly.

2 Grate the first three cheeses on the coarse side of a grater and stir into the white sauce. It will melt the cheese.

6 Serve immediately, with the grated Parmesan passed separately.

Note Other cheeses you can add or substitute are Provolone, Fontina, Taleggio or Emmenthaler. Instead of Parmesan you could use Asiago. Macaroni or elbow macaroni can be substituted.

Mostaccioli con Quattro Formaggi

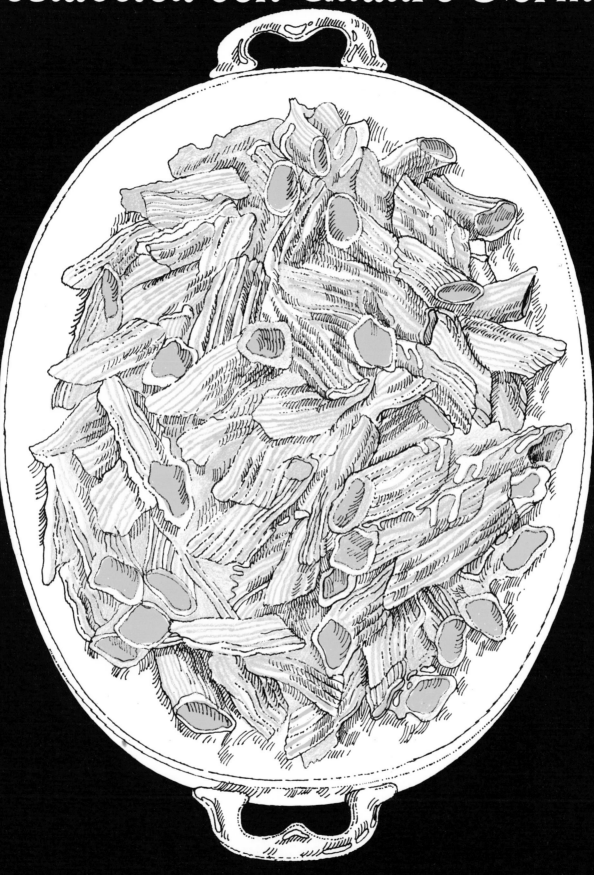

The most cheesy dish you ever tasted.
Full of creamy goodness, with a wonderful bite to it if you use mostaccioli, penne or rigatoni.
The cheese spills over into the holes, and you get twice the cheese with every bite. (Serves 4)

18–24 small clams *or* **tinned clams** *or* **mussels (fresh or tinned)**
7 tablespoons olive oil
3 cloves garlic, chopped into quarters
3 tablespoons chopped parsley
¼ teaspoon dried red pepper flakes
¼ teaspoon dried basil
2 shallots *or* **1 small onion, finely chopped**
200 ml (8 fl oz) white wine
400 gm (1 lb) linguine

5 Remove the clams with a slotted spoon onto a plate and leave to cool slightly. Remove the clams from their shells and cut them into quarters. Put them back into the sauce.

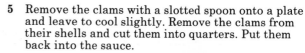

1 Scrub the clams well with a stiff brush, until all traces of sand have disappeared. You may want to soak them in cold water for a while. Rinse well.

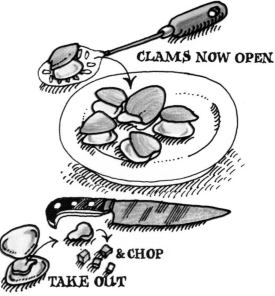

2 Heat the oil in a large saucepan, wide enough to accommodate the clams. Put in the garlic quarters and heat them through without browning, just for a minute or two. Remove the garlic with a slotted spoon.

6 Cook the linguine in plenty of boiling water (add salt when boiling) until *al dente*. Drain well.

3 To the oil add the parsley, red pepper flakes, basil and shallots or onions and sauté over medium heat, stirring frequently, for about 3 minutes.

4 Add the wine and all the clams, cover and leave to simmer for 7 minutes. After 7 minutes tilt the pot back and forth a few times to release the clam juices into the wine. Uncover.

7 Transfer the linguine onto a platter and spoon the clam sauce on top.

Serve immediately, no cheese!

Note If using canned, minced clams follow stages 2 and 3 but at stage 4 use only half the wine and 100 gm (4 oz) of bottled clam juice. Then add the clams and all their juice and cook, uncovered, for 8–10 minutes to reduce the liquid somewhat. Proceed with stages 6 and 7. If clams are unavailable, substitute 4 pints of fresh mussels for the clams. Instead of linguine you can use spaghetti.

LINGUINE CON VONGOLE

A slightly extravagant seafood dish but worth making if you
can obtain the clams. If you cannot, tinned clams or mussels can be used instead.
The clam juice, combined with the wine and herbs
produces a beautiful taste and aroma. Serves 6 as an hors d'oeuvre, or 4 as a main course.

1 800 gm–1·2 kilo (2–3 lb) chicken
about 1 litre (2 pints) cold water
1 teaspoon salt
25 gm (1 oz) butter
200 gm (8 oz) fresh mushrooms, sliced
50 gm (2 oz) butter
7 tablespoons flour
400 ml (16 fl oz) reserved chicken stock
200 ml (8 fl oz) milk
250 ml (½ pint) double cream
salt and pepper to taste
200–300 gm (8–12 oz) vermicelli
4 tablespoons dry breadcrumbs
4 tablespoons grated Parmesan cheese

16 fl. oz reserved stock

3 Melt the 50 gm (2 oz) butter in
another saucepan and when melted
stir in the flour. Mix well with
a wooden spoon or wire whisk and stir in the reserved stock and the milk.

Cook this mixture over a medium heat until it boils,
then leave to simmer, stirring all the time, for 3 minutes.
Remove from heat and stir in the cream, salt and pepper.
Add the reserved chicken pieces and the reserved
mushrooms.

VERMICELLI

1 Boil the chicken in salted water until tender, about
40–50 minutes. Remove the chicken, (place on a plate)
and leave to cool slightly. Reserve 400 ml (16 fl oz)
of the cooking water to use as stock. When the chicken
has cooled, skin and bone it carefully and cut the meat
into bite-sized pieces. Reserve the chopped meat as well.

2 Melt the 25 gm (1 oz) butter in a saucepan and sauté
the mushrooms until tender, stirring frequently.

4 Cook the vermicelli in plenty of boiling water
(add salt when boiling) until *al dente*. Drain.

5 Butter a large casserole or ovenproof baking dish. Combine the
sauce and the pasta thoroughly and pour the mixture
into the dish. Smooth the top with the back of a spoon.

6 Sprinkle the crumbs and grated cheese on top, and bake the dish, uncovered, in an oven preheated to 375°F, gas 5 (190°C) for 20–30
minutes. Serve more grated cheese separately.

Note This dish can be made up to 2 hours in advance up to stage 5. Keep
covered with foil or plastic wrap until ready to bake. Thin spaghetti
or regular spaghetti can be substituted for vermicelli.

Vermicelli e Pollo

A magnificently smooth, creamy dish. Very attractive and mouth-watering, so subtle it almost melts on the tongue. A luxurious lunch or dinner at a reasonable price. Great as a main course for 4, with a tossed salad and a glass of white wine. Bravo!

1 recipe egg-noodle dough, cut into cannelloni
  or 1 packet of bought cannelloni
1 medium onion chopped
2 tablespoons oil
1 clove garlic, chopped
400 gm (1 lb) minced beef
1 packet frozen spinach (or 400 gm [1 lb] fresh
  spinach), cooked and chopped
2 beaten eggs
5 tablespoons grated Parmesan cheese
3 tablespoons cream *or* evaporated milk
salt, pepper and oregano to taste
more Parmesan to taste
1 recipe Basciamella Sauce
1 recipe Tomato Sauce

5 In a bowl thoroughly combine with a fork the beef mixture, spinach, eggs, grated Parmesan, cream, salt, pepper and oregano. Mix it all up with a fork until well blended.

1 Boil the pasta pieces, a few at a time, in plenty of boiling water (add salt when boiling) until *al dente*. Drain and leave to cool slightly.

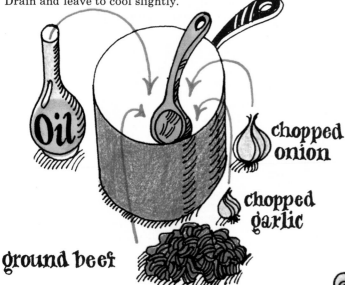

Oil

chopped onion

chopped garlic

ground beef

2 Sauté the chopped onion in the oil until soft and transparent. Add the garlic and sauté 1 minute longer.

3 Add the beef, breaking up any lumps with a wooden spoon, until it is brown and crumbly.

4 Cook the spinach according to the directions on the packet, drain well and leave to cool a little.

6 If using homemade squares of dough: Place one heaped teaspoon of this filling on each square of pasta. Fold both sides towards the middle, and place each cannelloni seam side down in a baking dish which has a thin layer of tomato sauce in it. Don't crowd them, or they will stick together.
Bought cannelloni can be filled with a teaspoon.
Place cannelloni in a single layer all over the baking dish. (Scatter leftover filling over them.)

store-bought

home made

Besciamella

7 Distribute the Besciamella evenly over the cannelloni. Then cover the Besciamella layer with the rest of the tomato sauce, and sprinkle with grated cheese.

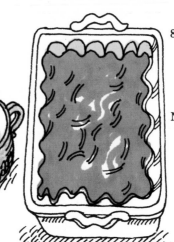

8 Bake in an oven preheated to 375°F, gas 5 (190°C) for 20 minutes if you are baking the dish straight away. If it has been allowed to get cold, bake it for 40 minutes.

Note

This dish can be made up to stage 7 two to three hours in advance. Keep covered with foil or plastic wrap until ready to bake.

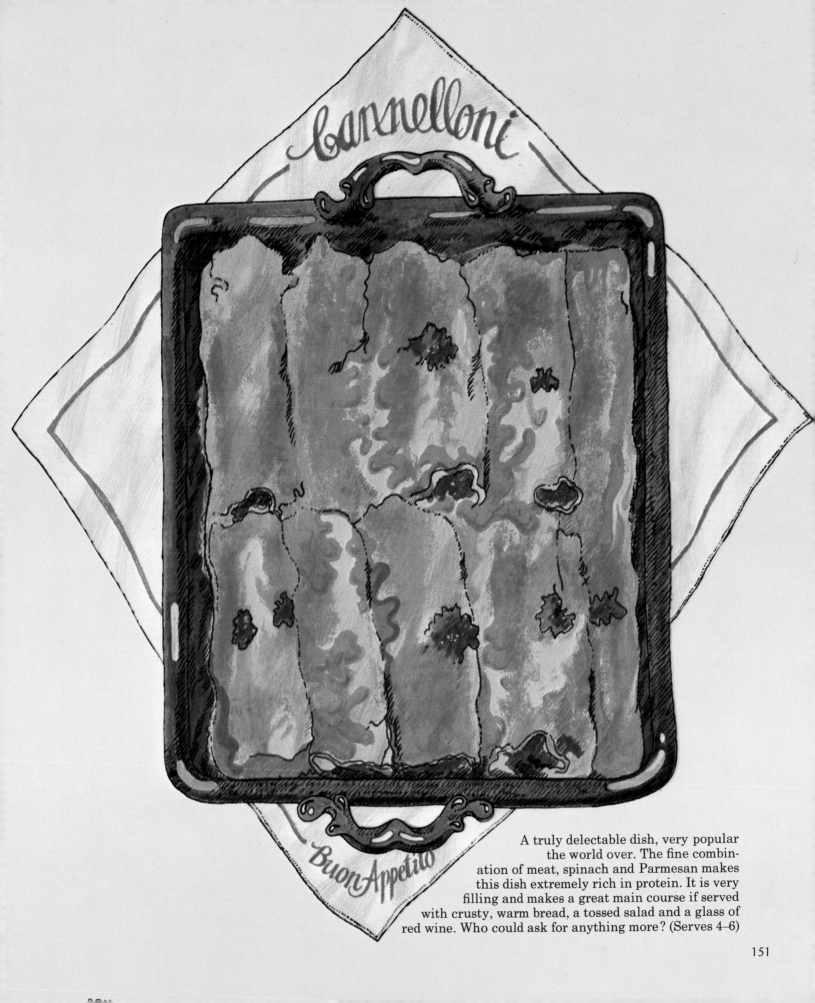

A truly delectable dish, very popular the world over. The fine combination of meat, spinach and Parmesan makes this dish extremely rich in protein. It is very filling and makes a great main course if served with crusty, warm bread, a tossed salad and a glass of red wine. Who could ask for anything more? (Serves 4–6)

151

37 gm (1½ oz) butter
1 tin tuna in oil (about 150–175 gm (6–7 oz))
2 tablespoons finely chopped parsley
200 ml (8 fl oz) double cream
salt and pepper to taste
200 gm (8 oz) margherita

3 Cook the margherita in plenty of boiling water
   (add salt when boiling) until *al dente*.
   Drain thoroughly.

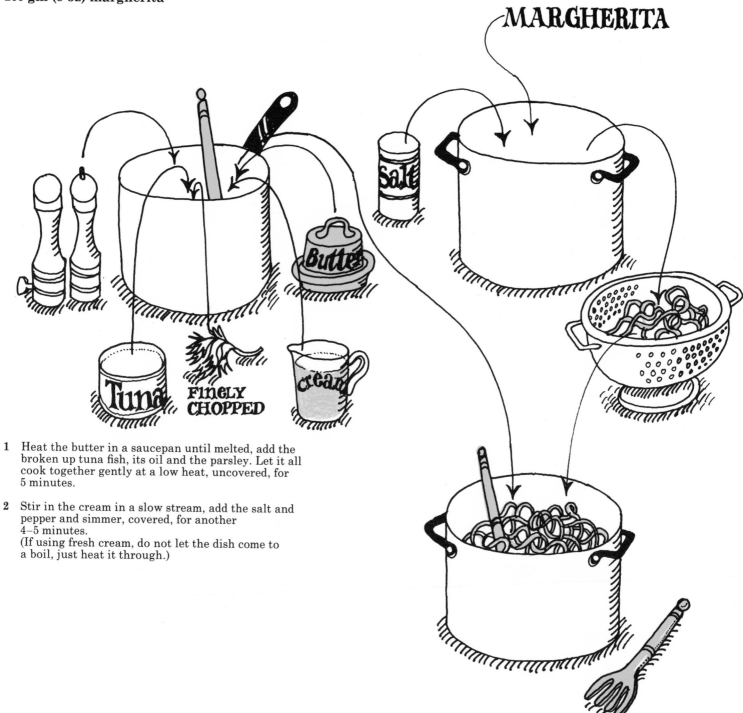

MARGHERITA

1 Heat the butter in a saucepan until melted, add the
   broken up tuna fish, its oil and the parsley. Let it all
   cook together gently at a low heat, uncovered, for
   5 minutes.

2 Stir in the cream in a slow stream, add the salt and
   pepper and simmer, covered, for another
   4–5 minutes.
   (If using fresh cream, do not let the dish come to
   a boil, just heat it through.)

4 Mix the margherita with the tuna sauce, preferably using
   two wooden forks, until well blended.

   Serve immediately.

Note Tagliatelle or fettuccine can be substituted for margherita.

MARGHERITA CON TONNO

An extremely piquant pasta dish, smooth, creamy and delicate. Very easy to prepare, fairly inexpensive to make and a good way to impress friends when you are in a hurry.

And it is just what children like, tuna fish and noodles. This dish serves 2 as a delightful lunch, or 4 as an hors d'oeuvre.

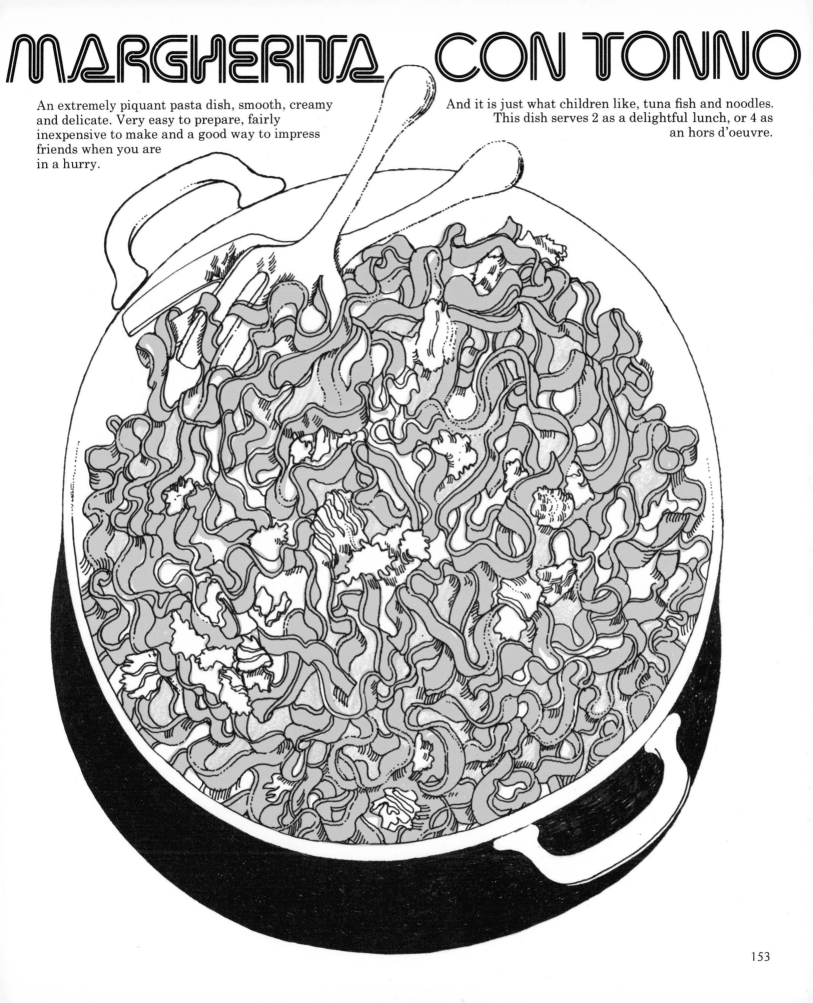

1 onion, finely chopped
3 tablespoons oil
2 cloves garlic, crushed
1·2 kilo (3 lb) fresh tomatoes,
  skinned and chopped
salt and pepper to taste
1 teaspoon sugar
½ teaspoon dried basil *or* tarragon
400 g (1 lb) raw shrimp, peeled
200 ml (8 fl oz) white wine
2 tablespoons chopped parsley
400 g (1 lb) linguine

1 Sauté the onion in the oil until soft
   and transparent. Add the garlic and
   sauté another 1 minute.

Oil   Finely chopped   CHOPPED   sugar   S   P   Basil   SKIN & CHOP

2 Add the tomatoes to the onions in the saucepan, together with
   the salt, pepper, sugar and basil or tarragon. Simmer slowly,
   uncovered, for 20 minutes.

3 Meanwhile, in another saucepan, simmer the peeled shrimp in
   the wine for 3–4 minutes. Add them to the tomatoes when the
   tomatoes are cooked. Also
   add the chopped parsley and
   let it simmer another
   4–5 minutes.

White wine

4 Boil the linguine in plenty of boiling water (add
   salt when boiling) until *al dente*. Drain.

Salt   linguine   Drain

5 Mix the linguine and the shrimp sauce until well combined. Divide the pasta into six individual small
   dishes and spoon any sauce that has accumulated in
   the bottom of the saucepan over the pasta.

   Serve immediately.

Note   Use only raw shrimp for this dish.
           Spaghetti can be substituted for linguine.

154

Linguine alla Marinara

Buon Appetito

The super seafood
taste of the shrimp gives this
dish a flavour particularly distinctive
of the Adriatic coast. The fresh tomatoes add colour and gusto. It is the
range of summer tastes which makes this dish especially pleasant as an hors d'oeuvre.
(Serves 6)

1 recipe green-noodle dough
   cut into tagliatelle
   or **300 gm (12 oz) bought green noodles**
150 gm (4–6 oz) soft butter
1–3 cloves garlic, crushed
8 tablespoons grated Parmesan cheese
black pepper and salt to taste

1 Boil the noodles in plenty of water (add salt
when boiling) until *al dente*. Drain.

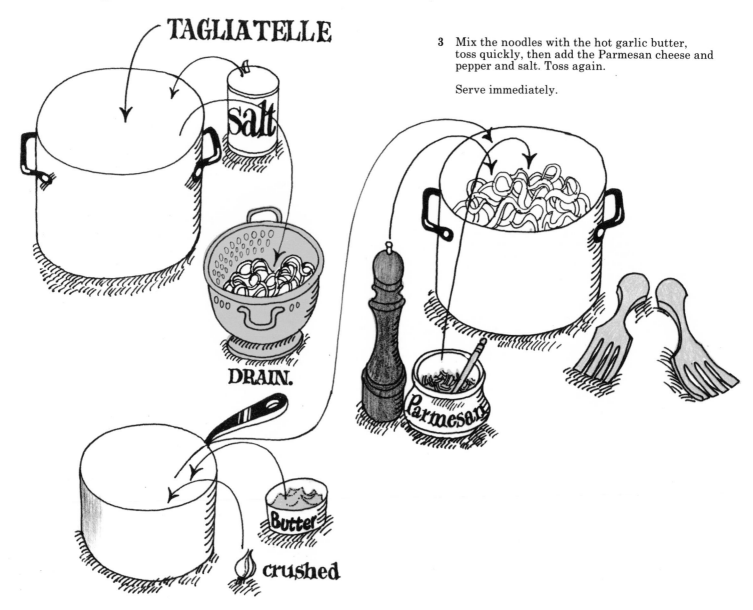

TAGLIATELLE

salt

DRAIN.

Butter

crushed

Parmesan

3 Mix the noodles with the hot garlic butter,
toss quickly, then add the Parmesan cheese and
pepper and salt. Toss again.

Serve immediately.

2 While the pasta is cooking, heat the butter in another
saucepan and sauté the garlic in it over a very low heat.
Do not let either the butter or the garlic brown.
Sauté it for only a minute.

Note This recipe is especially good
with homemade green noodles.

TAGLIATELLE VERDI CON AGLIO

One of those melt-in-the-mouth pasta dishes. Incredibly smooth and creamy, with a glorious colour. With a mild or strong garlic flavour, whichever you prefer. A marvellous first course for 4–5, or a great side dish with fried, roast or grilled meat.

600 gm (1½ lb) ricotta cheese
2 beaten eggs
3 tablespoons finely chopped parsley
2 tablespoons grated Parmesan *or* Romano cheese
50 gm (2 oz) grated mozzarella cheese
1 recipe egg noodle dough
  cut into manicotti,
    or 1 packet bought manicotti
double the recipe for Tomato Sauce
5 tablespoons grated cheese

1 Drain the ricotta cheese well.

2 Place the ricotta in a mixing bowl, add
the eggs, parsley, nutmeg and the grated cheeses.
Blend well with a fork.

3 Cook the manicotti in plenty of boiling water (add
salt when boiling) until *al dente*. (Cook a few at a time.)
Drain and leave to cool slightly.

4 If using homemade pasta squares, place a heaped tablespoon of filling
on each rectangle, then fold both sides towards the middle, to cover
the filling. (Bought manicotti can be filled with a teaspoon.)

**homemade
square**

store~bought

5 Spread a thin layer of the tomato sauce on
the bottom of a buttered, ovenproof baking
dish. Lay the manicotti, seam side down,
and not touching, in a single layer in the
dish. Pour the rest of the tomato sauce over
the top.

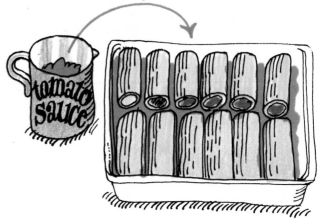

6 Sprinkle the Parmesan cheese on top and bake the dish, uncovered,
in an oven preheated to 375°F, gas 5 (170°C) for about 30 minutes.

Note This dish can be made up to 2 hours in advance up to
stage 5. Keep the dish covered with foil or plastic
wrap until ready to put it in the oven.

Manicotti

In its outward appearance manicotti vaguely resembles
cannelloni. However, that is the extent of the similarity. Manicotti oozes
the taste of a savoury cheese filling, topped with a delicious tomato sauce.
Extremely satisfying, very Italian and very appetizing. (Serves 4–6)

2 tablespoons oil
1 large onion, finely chopped
1–2 cloves garlic, crushed (optional)
1 green pepper, cut into strips
black pepper to taste
dried tarragon to taste
1 recipe tomato sauce
400 gm (1 lb) cod *or* **sole** *or* **haddock, cubed**
400 gm (1 lb) tagliatelle

1 Heat the oil in a heavy saucepan, then add the chopped onion, crushed garlic, green pepper strips and sauté it all until soft, about 8 minutes. Then add the black pepper and tarragon.

3 Cook the tagliatelle in plenty of boiling water (add salt when boiling) until *al dente*. Drain.

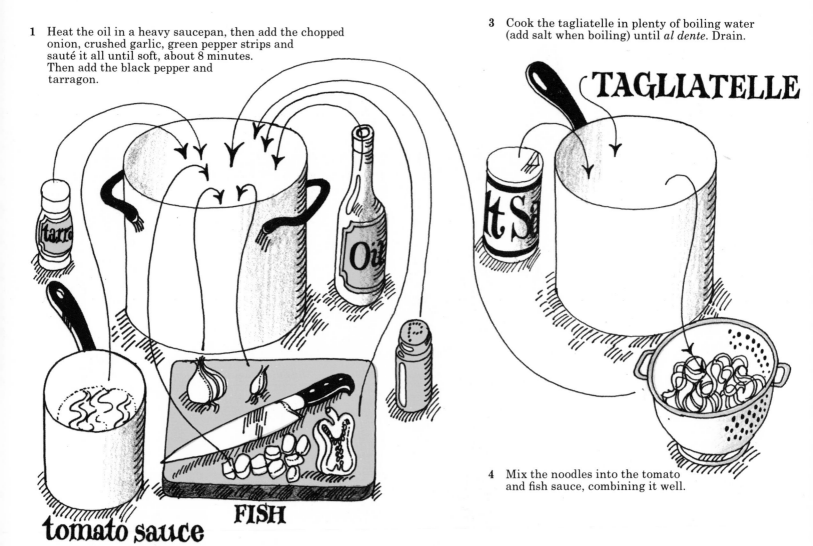

TAGLIATELLE

tomato sauce

FISH

4 Mix the noodles into the tomato and fish sauce, combining it well.

2 To the saucepan add the tomato sauce and the chunks of fish. Cook the dish, uncovered, for about 10 minutes, until the fish is tender but not falling apart.

Tagliatelle e Pesce

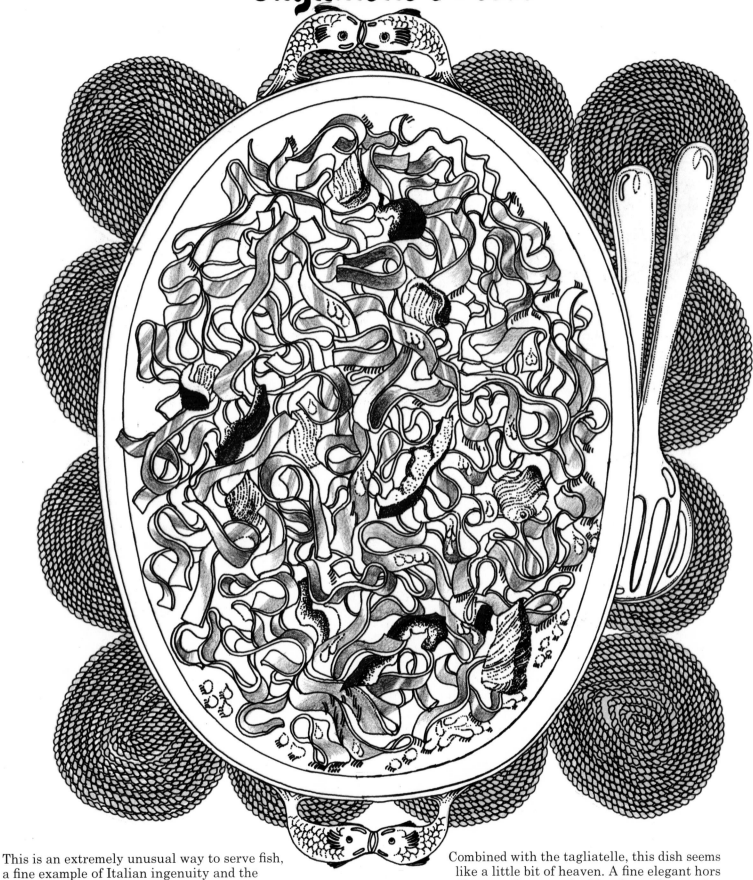

This is an extremely unusual way to serve fish, a fine example of Italian ingenuity and the versatility of pasta. Fresh chunks of fish bathed in a delicate, delicious tomato sauce. Combined with the tagliatelle, this dish seems like a little bit of heaven. A fine elegant hors d'oeuvre if you are looking for an impressive and unusual fish course for 6. Buon Appetito!

37 gm (1½ oz) butter
400 gm (1 lb) fresh mushrooms,
    whole if small, sliced
    if large
2 tablespoons oil
400 gm (1 lb) minced pork
1–2 cloves garlic, crushed
½ teaspoon dried basil
½ teaspoon dried oregano

salt and pepper to taste
100 ml (4 fl oz) white wine
2 tablespoons flour
3 tablespoons tomato purée
200 ml (8 fl oz) beef stock
300 gm (12 oz) farfalloni
freshly grated Parmesan
    cheese

4   Add the tomato purée, and the stock. Stir well, cover, and leave to simmer over a low flame for about 25 minutes. Stir quite often. When done, add the reserved mushrooms.

1   In a saucepan melt the butter and over medium heat sauté the mushrooms until cooked, stirring often. Set aside.

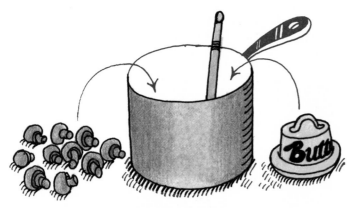

FARFALLONI

2   In another saucepan heat the oil and brown the pork in it, breaking up any lumps with a wooden spoon. At this point I like to pour off all the accumulated fat. Stir into the meat the garlic, basil, oregano, salt and pepper. Leave to cook for 2 minutes.

5   Cook the farfalloni in plenty of boiling water (add salt when boiling) until *al dente*. Drain.

6   Mix together the farfalloni and the meat-mushroom sauce and serve immediately. Pass the grated Parmesan separately.

Note   This sauce can be made hours in advance, just re-heat it while the pasta is cooking.
This dish is also good when made with egg noodles of any width.

3   Turn up the heat and pour in the wine. Let it boil rapidly until the foam subsides. Then stir in all the flour, stirring well.

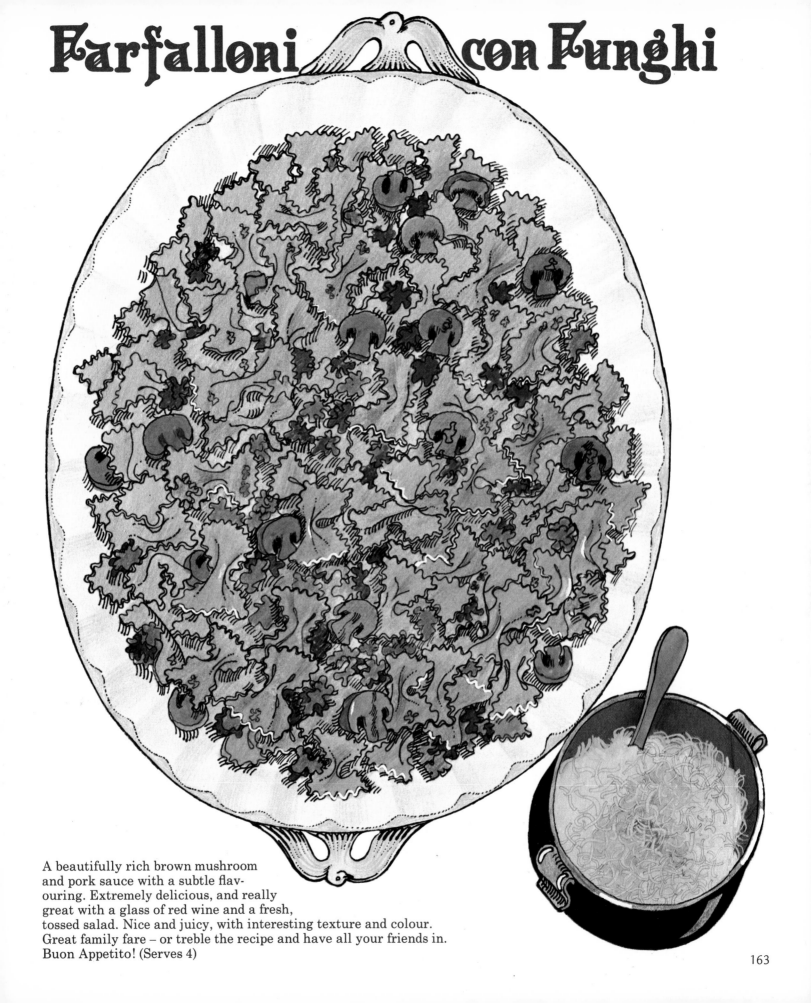

Farfalloni con Funghi

A beautifully rich brown mushroom
and pork sauce with a subtle flav-
ouring. Extremely delicious, and really
great with a glass of red wine and a fresh,
tossed salad. Nice and juicy, with interesting texture and colour.
Great family fare – or treble the recipe and have all your friends in.
Buon Appetito! (Serves 4)

300 gm (12 oz) fettuccine
100 ml (4 fl oz) double cream
50–75 gm (2–4 oz) softened butter
8 tablespoons grated Parmesan cheese
150 gm (6 oz) fresh or frozen peas, cooked
200 gm (8 oz) prosciutto *or* boiled ham,
  cut into thin strips
black pepper to taste

3   Drain the fettuccine, pour them back into the
    pot and quickly toss in the flaked soft butter
    and the Parmesan.

1   Cook the fettuccine in plenty of boiling water (add salt
    when boiling) until *al dente*.

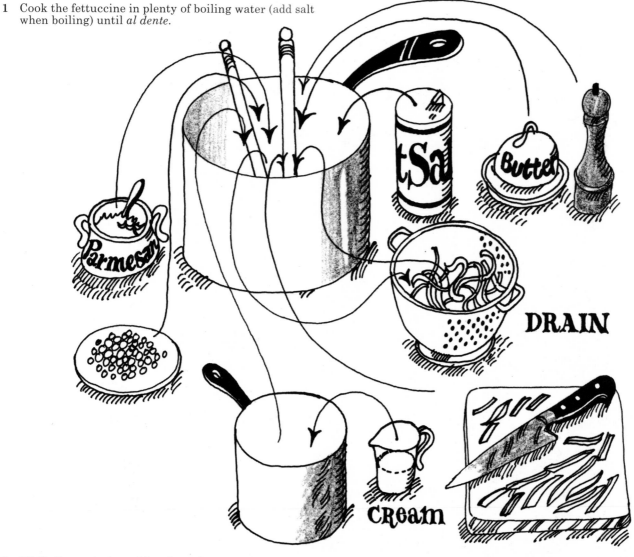

DRAIN

CREAM

2   While the pasta is cooking, heat the cream
    in a small saucepan.

4   Add the hot cream, the peas, the prosciutto
    and black pepper and toss again.

    Serve immediately.

Fettuccine alla Romana

A deliciously creamy, colourful dish, the way it is served in Rome.
One of our many favourites, just too good for words. Super for a quick lunch.
Invite your friends, bring out the wine and the good conversation.
Buon Appetito. (Serves 4)

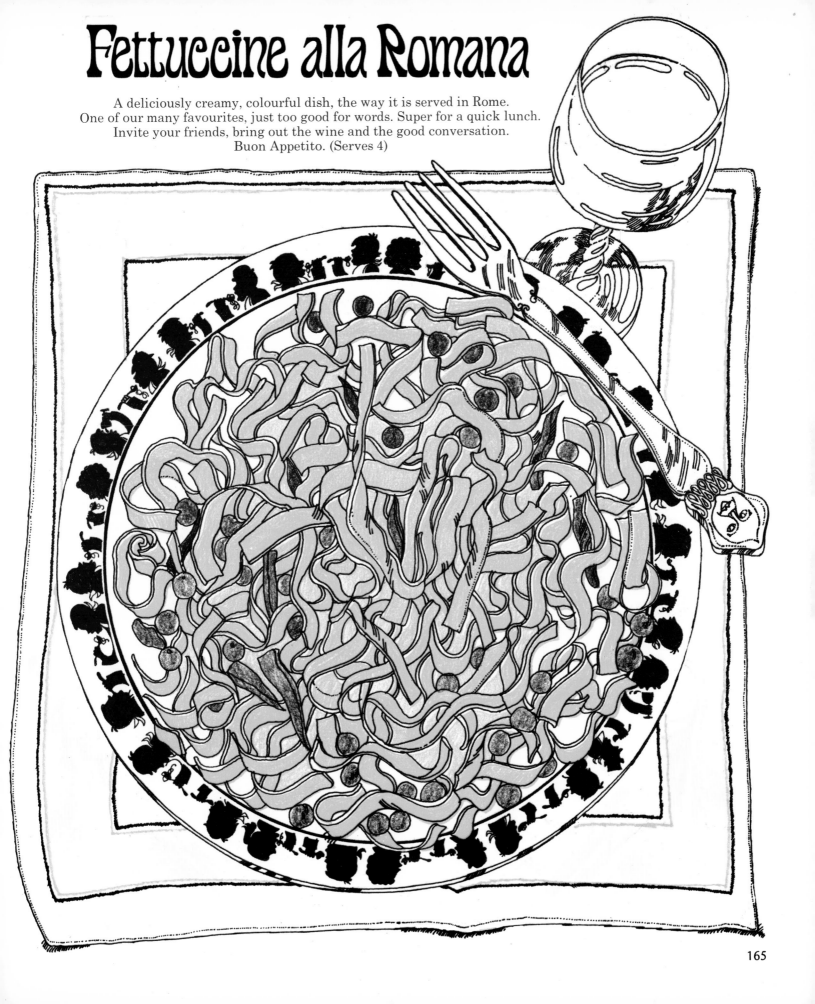

2 tablespoons oil
1 onion, finely chopped
1 red pepper (green if red is unavailable) cut into strips
1 clove garlic, chopped
1 tablespoon chopped parsley
200 gm (8 oz) lean bacon, cut into strips
400 gm (1 lb) fresh tomatoes, peeled and roughly chopped
   or one 400 gm (1 lb) tin tomatoes
generous grating of black pepper
300 gm (12 oz) spaghetti
2 tablespoons oil
4 tablespoons grated Parmesan *or* Romano cheese

1   Heat the oil in a saucepan and add the onion, red or green
    pepper, garlic, parsley and bacon. Sauté for about 5 minutes,
    uncovered and stirring often.

2   To this mixture add the tomatoes and pepper. Simmer this dish,
    uncovered, for 15 minutes. Add a little salt then if necessary.

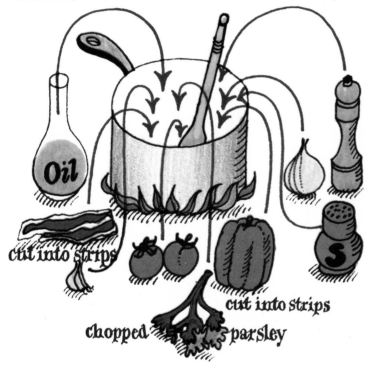

4   Place the spaghetti in a hot bowl,
    sprinkle on the oil and cheese and toss well.

3   Cook the spaghetti in plenty of boiling water
    (add salt when boiling) until *al dente*. Drain.

5   Serve the pasta in individual small bowls,
    with the sauce spooned on top.

    Serve immediately.

Note   The sauce itself can be made several hours in advance
       and re-heated.

166

Spaghetti all'Amatriciana

Spaghetti All'Amatriciana takes its name from Amatrice,
a small town north of Rome, famous because generations
of grocers came from there. Full-bodied and robust taste,
a juicy blend of pasta, vegetables, meat and cheese.
A great light lunch for 3 or 4, or an hors d'oeuvre
for 5 or 6.

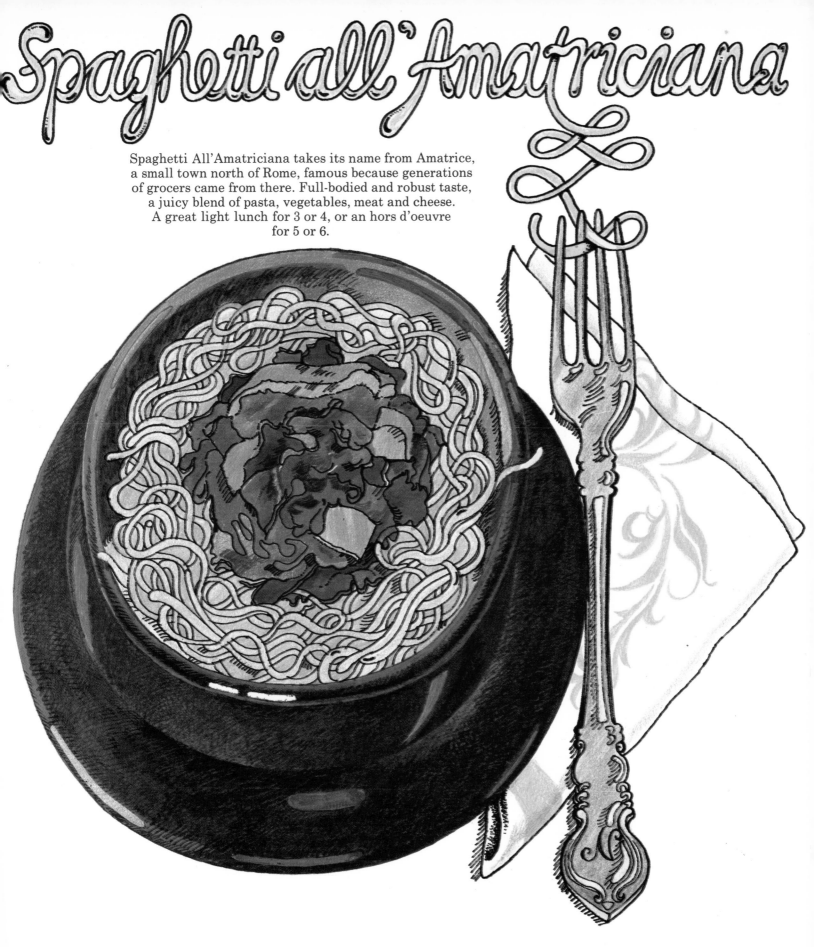

1 medium-sized aubergine
salt
6 medium-sized tomatoes, skinned,
deseeded and chopped
1–2 cloves garlic, crushed
1–2 tablespoons parsley, chopped
½ teaspoon dried red pepper flakes
25 gm (1 oz) butter
enough oil for frying aubergine
400 gm (1 lb) spaghetti

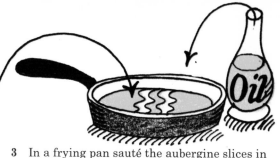

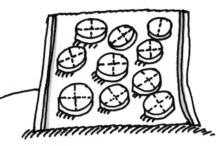

3   In a frying pan sauté the aubergine slices in some hot oil. They will absorb the oil quite quickly, so keep adding more oil as needed. Fry the slices till they are golden brown on both sides.

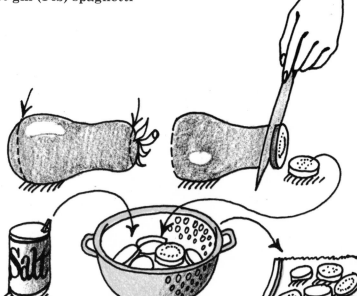

4   Drain the slices on paper towels to absorb the excess fat, then cut them into halves or quarters, and add them to the tomato sauce. Heat through again while the pasta is cooking. Taste for seasoning.

5   Cook the spaghetti in plenty of boiling water (add salt when boiling) until *al dente*. Drain.

1   Cut off both ends of the aubergine and cut the remaining piece into 6 mm (¼ inch) thick slices. Put the slices into a non-metal bowl, sprinkle a little salt on them, and leave to drain for 30–45 minutes. After that dry them thoroughly with paper towels.

SPAGHETTI

crushed   chopped

chopped

2   Meanwhile sauté the chopped tomatoes, garlic, parsley and red pepper flakes in the butter in another saucepan for about 5 minutes. Reserve.

6   Serve the pasta on individual hot plates, with the sauce spooned on top.

A delightful light summer lunch. Colourful and unusual.
You can taste the summer goodness of fresh vegetables,
a truly Sicilian combination of tastes.
The more you eat it, the more you will like it.
(Serves 4)

1 recipe egg-noodle dough
400 gm (1 lb) ricotta cheese
50 gm (2 oz) Parmesan cheese, grated
3 tablespoons chopped parsley
little salt and pepper
1 medium egg

little grated nutmeg
1 recipe Ragù di Manzo, *or* Ragù Bolognese
   or Salsa di Pomodori
   or just melted butter and Parmesan
grated Parmesan cheese

1   Prepare the filling by combining in a bowl the ricotta, Parmesan, parsley, salt, pepper, egg and nutmeg. Blend it well together with a fork.

5   Place the finished tortellini in a single layer (not allowing them to touch) on a well floured wax paper or greaseproof paper and proceed to shape the rest.

6   Boil the tortellini, a few at a time, in plenty of boiling water (add salt when boiling) until *al dente*. Drain well.

2   Roll out the dough to 2 mm ($\frac{1}{8}$ inch) thickness. Cut the dough into 50-mm (2-inch) circles, with a biscuit-cutter or glass of that diameter.

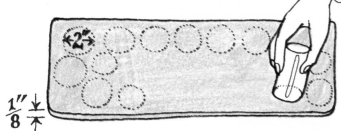

$\frac{1''}{8}$

3   Place about $\frac{1}{2}$ teaspoon of filling on each circle.

7   Serve them hot, with one of the sauces spooned on top. Pass plenty of grated Parmesan cheese separately.

Note   You can make tortellini a few hours ahead. Keep them on a well floured tray, not touching one another, and dust them heavily with flour. Keep refrigerated until ready to boil.

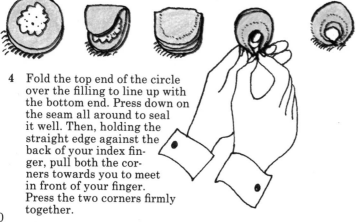

4   Fold the top end of the circle over the filling to line up with the bottom end. Press down on the seam all around to seal it well. Then, holding the straight edge against the back of your index finger, pull both the corners towards you to meet in front of your finger. Press the two corners firmly together.

Tortellini

One of the glorious stuffed pasta dishes. When served without a meat sauce they are called Tortellini da Vigilia (lean tortellini). They are served thus on religious holidays, when the eating of meat is not permitted. (Serves 6 as an hors d'oeuvre, 4 as a main course.)

400 gm (1 lb) lean lamb, cubed
salt and pepper to taste
¼ teaspoon dried rosemary
3 tablespoons oil
1–2 cloves garlic, chopped
75 ml (3 fl oz) white wine
400 gm (1 lb) fresh tomatoes,
  skinned and chopped
150–200 ml (6–8 fl oz) beef stock
200 gm (8 oz) cavatelli
grated Parmesan cheese

1 Season the lamb cubes with a little salt, pepper and rosemary.

2 Heat the oil in a saucepan over fairly high heat and brown the meat-cubes on all sides. Add the garlic and cook 1 minute longer.

3 Pour the wine over the meat and let it boil, uncovered, until the foam subsides.

4 Stir in the tomatoes and stock and simmer, only partially covered, for 1–1½ hours. Stir frequently. The sauce will reduce to about half and be fairly thick. Adjust seasoning.

5 Cook the cavatelli in plenty of boiling water (add salt when boiling) until *al dente*. Drain.

CAVATELLI

6 Combine the pasta and the sauce, then stir in the Parmesan cheese.

   Serve immediately, with plenty of freshly grated Parmesan passed separately.

Note Instead of cavatelli you can use macaroni, rotini, mostaccioli, rigatoni, conchiglie or farfalloni.

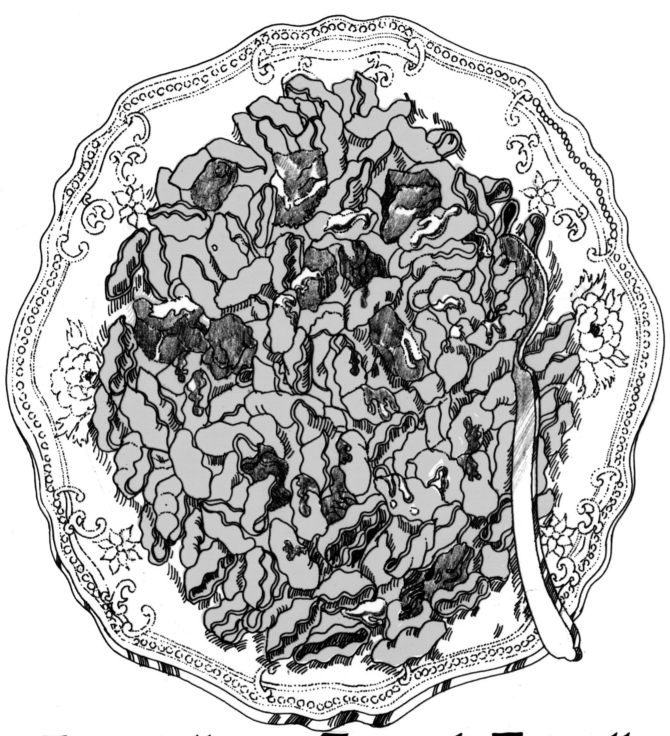

Cavatelli con Sugo di Agnello

Country character is what makes this dish so hearty and delightful.
The succulent pieces of lamb combine extremely well with the rich tomato sauce,
which in turn complements this unusual pasta shape. Great family fare.
(Serves 3–4)

Sauces

Salsa di Pomodori
(Basic Tomato Sauce)

1 large onion, chopped
2 tablespoons oil
1 clove garlic, chopped (optional)
1 large (800 gm [2 lb]) tin tomatoes
or 800 gm (2 lb) fresh tomatoes, skinned and chopped
3 level tablespoons tomato purée
1 teaspoon dried basil
½ teaspoon sugar
salt and pepper to taste

Sauté onion in oil until soft and transparent. Do not let the onion brown. Add the garlic (if used) and sauté one minute. Stir in the tomatoes and juice, breaking them up with a wooden spoon. Add the tomato purée, basil, sugar and a pinch of salt and pepper. Simmer the sauce, partially covered, for 30–40 minutes, until it has reduced to a thick consistency which will coat the back of a spoon. Stir sauce often to prevent burning. Strain it through a fine sieve, pressing down hard on the tomatoes and onions. Add more salt and pepper if needed. This makes about 400 ml (16 fl oz) of sauce which can be used over any kind of pasta, or in baked dishes. It will keep for weeks, tightly covered, in the refrigerator, so you can make a large quantity and use some when needed.

Ragù di Manzo
(Beef Sauce)

1 large onion, finely chopped
2 tablespoons oil
1–3 cloves garlic, crushed (optional)
400 gm (1 lb) minced beef
1 400 gm (1 lb) tin tomatoes
or 400 gm (1 lb) fresh tomatoes, skinned and chopped
2 tablespoons tomato purée
1 teaspoon dried oregano
1 teaspoon dried basil
1 bay leaf
salt and pepper to taste
75–100 ml (3–4 fl oz) red wine

Sauté onion in oil until soft and transparent. Add garlic and cook another minute. Add minced beef and cook it until brown and crumbly. Break up any lumps with a wooden spoon. Pour off accumulated fat. Stir in tomatoes, breaking them up with a wooden spoon, tomato purée, oregano, basil, bay leaf, and a little salt and pepper. Simmer the sauce, partially covered, stirring often, for 30–40 minutes. Before serving, stir in the wine off the heat. Serve this sauce over any pasta, and serve plenty of grated Parmesan with it.

Marinara Sauce

3 tablespoons oil
1 large onion, chopped
1 small carrot, chopped
1–2 cloves garlic, crushed
1 800 gm (2 lb) tin tomatoes
or 800 gm (2 lb) fresh tomatoes, skinned and chopped
1 teaspoon dried oregano
½ teaspoon dried basil
salt and pepper to taste

Sauté in oil, the onion, carrot and garlic for about 5 minutes. Add the tomatoes, breaking them up with a wooden spoon. Add the oregano and basil and simmer partially covered, for about 30 minutes. Strain sauce through a fine sieve, pushing down hard on the vegetables. Reheat if necessary, or, if the sauce is too thin, boil it down, uncovered, over a medium heat, until it has reduced to the desired consistency. Season with salt and pepper to taste. This sauce can be served over any kind of pasta.

Ragù Bolognese
(Bolognese Sauce)

37 gm (1½ oz) butter
4 rashers bacon, cut into strips
1 large onion, finely chopped
1 medium carrot, finely chopped
1 stalk celery, finely chopped
2 tablespoons oil
130 gm (⅓ lb) minced beef
130 gm (⅓ lb) minced pork
130 gm (⅓ lb) minced veal
100 ml (4 fl oz) white wine
500 ml (1 pint) beef stock
3 tablespoons tomato purée
1 teaspoon dried oregano
little grated nutmeg
salt and pepper to taste
250 ml (½ pint) double cream (optional)

Melt butter in a frying pan and in it sauté the bacon, onion, carrot and celery. Cook, uncovered, stirring often, for about 10 minutes. Set aside till needed. Heat the oil in another saucepan and in it brown the meats, breaking up any lumps with a wooden spoon, until the mixture is brown and crumbly. Pour off fat (see page 11). Stir in wine over medium high heat letting most of it evaporate. Stir in beef stock, tomato purée, oregano, nutmeg, and a little salt and pepper. Add reserved vegetables and bacon. Simmer sauce, partially covered, until it has reduced to a thick sauce, about 40–60 minutes. Add all or some of the cream, if liked. When served over pasta this sauce rounds off the flavours.

Besciamella
(Bechamel Sauce)

75 gm (3 oz) butter
4 tablespoons flour
625 ml (1¼ pints) milk
salt and pepper to taste
little ground nutmeg

Melt the butter in a saucepan. Make a roux by adding the flour, and stirring with a wire whisk until the flour has been absorbed by the butter. Do not let it brown! Slowly add the milk, stirring quickly and constantly with a wire whisk. Raise the heat, stirring all the time, until the sauce comes to the boil and thickens. Cook, uncovered, still stirring, for 3 minutes. Season with salt, pepper and nutmeg. This sauce is used in many baked pasta dishes.

Pesto all Genovese
(Genoese Pesto)

1–3 cloves garlic
a quantity of fresh basil (leaves only)
50–75 gm (2–3 oz) grated Parmesan *or* Romano cheese
2 tablespoons finely chopped pine nuts
or almonds (optional)
salt and pepper to taste
250 ml (10 fl oz) olive oil

Mash garlic and basil to a smooth paste with a mortar and pestle, or use a bowl and the back of a spoon. Add cheese and nuts (if used) and press them down. Mix in the salt and pepper. Whisk in the oil slowly, in an even stream. The sauce should be very smooth. This sauce can also be made in a mixer. Blend all ingredients except cheese at high speed, until sauce is smooth and fairly thick. Pour into a bowl. If sauce is too thick, thin down with some oil as required. Blend in the cheese. This sauce can be served over any pasta dish.

INDEX